INTERNET TO GO

INTERNET
To Go

Alan Simpson

²GO™

SAN FRANCISCO ► PARIS ► DÜSSELDORF ► SOEST ► LONDON

Associate Publisher: Gary Masters
Contracts and Licensing Manager: Kristine O'Callaghan
Acquisitions Editor: Gary Masters
Developmental Editors: Davina Baum, Ed Copony
Editor: Ed Copony
Technical Editor: Gary Masters
Book Designer: Maureen Forys, Happenstance Type-O-Rama
Graphic Illustrator: Chris Gillespie
Electronic Publishing Specialist: Maureen Forys, Happenstance Type-O-Rama
Production Team Leader: David Zielonka
Indexer: Nancy Guenther
Cover Designer: Ingalls + Associates
Cover Illustrator: Hank Osuna

To Susan, Ashley, and Alec, as always.

ACKNOWLEDGMENTS

Every book is a team effort, and this one is no exception. There are lots of people who deserve credit and to whom I owe a great deal of thanks.

At Sybex, I'd like to thank Gary Masters for presenting this opportunity to me. Also at Sybex, many thanks to Davina Baum, Developmental Editor, Ed Copony, Editor, David Zielonka, Production Team Leader, Maureen Forys, Desktop Publisher, and Chris Gillespie, Graphic Artist.

To Bill Gladstone, Matt Wagner, and the rest of the gang at Waterside Productions, many thanks for bringing this opportunity to me and working out all the details.

To Susan, Ashley, and Alec, thanks for hanging in there through yet another time-devouring Daddy project.

TABLE OF CONTENTS

INTRODUCTION

Welcome to *Internet To Go*, the quick and easy way to take advantage of the great (and free) Internet tools for Windows. Let's get straight to the important stuff.

Who This Book Is For

This book is written for people who don't know anything about the Internet. If you don't have a clue as to how to get your PC connected to the Internet, then you're in the right place: We start with the very first step of choosing and hooking up a modem.

You do need a PC to use this book. That PC should have either Windows 95 or Windows 98 on it, and you should already:

▶ Know how to point, click, double-click, and right-click

▶ Know how to open icons and menus

▶ Understand the basic concepts of *files* and *folders*

If any of that stuff is a mystery to you, then learning to do *anything* with your computer will be tough going. You'd be better off backing up and learning the basics first. If you use Windows 95, an introductory book like Bob Cowart's *Windows 95 Quick and Easy* or Sharon Crawford's *ABC's of Windows 95*, both published by Sybex, will do just fine. If you're using Windows 98, I recommend *Windows 98 To Go*. Like this book, that one is short, cheap, and will quickly teach you everything you need to know.

If you're using DOS, Windows 3.*x*, Linux, Unix, or a Mac, this book won't do you much good. You'd be better off finding a book that covers those particular machines or a more general book that tries to cover several machines. But be forewarned—books that cover the Internet without regard to the computer you're using can be very difficult to follow. They tend to cover a lot of theory without actually telling you how to *do* anything.

How to Use This Book

This is very much a *how-to* book. There are tons of step-by-step instructions and useful pictures everywhere, as you can see just by flipping through the pages. The goal here is to get you online and using the Internet productively as quickly as possible, without a bunch of technical ramblings and trite opinions.

Exactly how you use this book is entirely up to you. Here are some options:

- ▶ If you want the get on the Internet right now, to browse the Web and do e-mail, go to Appendix C. You could be browsing the Web in a matter of minutes.

- ▶ You could just keep the book by your bed and read a little each night before you doze off to kill two birds with one stone: You'll get hep to all the Internet buzz, and it'll cure your insomnia, too.

- ▶ If you're stuck on a jet with some time to kill or you don't have a computer handy, then just start reading Chapter 1. That'll provide a smooth tutorial that builds from the absolute basics up, avoiding the frustration that stems from trying to jump straight to the advanced stuff without understanding the basics.

What's Covered

To keep things simple, this book focuses on the Internet programs that Microsoft provides for free, including:

- ▶ The Internet Connection Wizard (to get connected)

- ▶ Microsoft Internet Explorer (to browse the Web)

- ▶ Microsoft Outlook Express (for E-mail, Newsgroups, and Mailing Lists)

▶ Microsoft NetMeeting (for talking, videoconferencing, and sharing documents on the Internet)

All these programs come free with Windows 98 and later versions of Windows 95. If you have an early version of Windows 95, you might not have all the programs. But once you're online and able to browse the Web, you can download any missing programs for free. This book will show you where to go and how to download files from the Internet.

In addition, this book covers many general topics to help you become Internet-savvy quickly, including:

▶ Choosing a modem and Internet Service Provider

▶ Tools and techniques for kid-safe surfing

▶ Quick solutions to common problems

▶ A glossary defining all the nerd terms you'll come across

Cool Features

This book has some features to make life easy for you. There is a table of contents up front and an index in back to help you look up information on an as-needed basis. There's also a glossary at the back of the book to help you translate Web jargon. The appendices provide quick solutions to common problems, resources for even more cool Internet programs, and top tips for the harried—an instant on-ramp to the Internet for those who are pressed for time.

Within each chapter, the following icons point out noteworthy tidbits of information:

NOTE
This is some noteworthy item. Perhaps a reminder or something to help you remember new information.

TIP

Especially helpful tips, tricks, and techniques are marked with this icon.

WARNING

This icon points out areas where you need to be cautious and think before you act. A mistake here could lead to major inconveniences later down the road. Fortunately, they're few and far between.

See you online!

Chapter 1

UNTANGLING THE NET

U nless you've been hiding under a rock somewhere for a long time, you probably know that the Internet is the biggest thing to hit the tech world in years. Everybody's using it for e-mail, shopping, news, stock trading, meeting people, getting answers to burning questions, and a whole lot more. If you find yourself overwhelmed by the sheer number of buzzwords and services offered—e-mail, World Wide Web, chats, secure online shopping, and so forth—don't feel bad. Even though there are millions of people using the Internet already, there are still tens of millions of people who just haven't had the time to join the crowd. So you're not alone. Hopefully by the time you finish reading this chapter, you'll have a clearer picture of how all the pieces fit together. I'll be brief because I know most of you are more interested in "doing" rather than "learning about" the Internet.

What Is the Internet?

In a nutshell, the Internet is a whole bunch of cables running around the entire globe, connecting millions of computers to each other. Technically, it's called a Wide Area Network, or WAN (rhymes with *pan*). The net (as it's also called) was originally conceived and built in the United States using taxpayer money. Which means that, if you're a taxpayer, you already own a part of it.

Even though you might connect to the Internet via telephone lines, the Internet is entirely separate from the phone system. There are no "long distance" charges like the phone company has. Whether you send an e-mail next door or halfway around the world, the cost is the same: zero dollars and zero cents. That's not to say that using the Internet is entirely free. You'll need to pay an Internet Service Provider fee to get you connected to the Internet (Chapter 3 explains the role of the ISP and cost issues in more detail).

The Internet shouldn't be confused with commercial services such as America Online, MSN, CompuServe, and Prodigy. Those services are private, and hence can maintain editorial control over the content they provide. They get to decide what's appropriate, and inappropriate, for their customers.

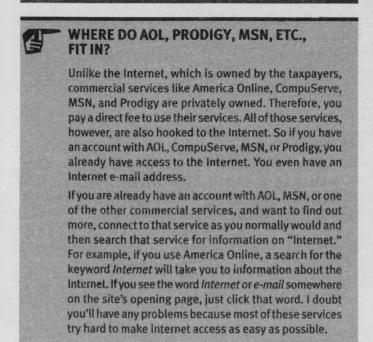

WHERE DO AOL, PRODIGY, MSN, ETC., FIT IN?

Unlike the Internet, which is owned by the taxpayers, commercial services like America Online, CompuServe, MSN, and Prodigy are privately owned. Therefore, you pay a direct fee to use their services. All of those services, however, are also hooked to the Internet. So if you have an account with AOL, CompuServe, MSN, or Prodigy, you already have access to the Internet. You even have an Internet e-mail address.

If you are already have an account with AOL, MSN, or one of the other commercial services, and want to find out more, connect to that service as you normally would and then search that service for information on "Internet." For example, if you use America Online, a search for the keyword *Internet* will take you to information about the Internet. If you see the word *Internet* or *e-mail* somewhere on the site's opening page, just click that word. I doubt you'll have any problems because most of these services try hard to make Internet access as easy as possible.

The Internet, on the other hand, is not owned or governed by anybody. And, in the U.S., it's protected by freedom of speech laws. Such protection means that the Internet isn't censored, so anything goes.

There are tons of family-friendly, useful Web sites, but there's also content out there that you really don't want your kids being exposed too. A thorny subject for parents. (As I know all too well, my own kids are aged 6 and 11.) Chapter 7 discusses strategies for protecting your kids from inappropriate content.

Services of the Internet

The Internet is one huge network that's divided up into several major services that it provides to its users. You may have heard of some of these services already—and been confused about how all the different pieces fit together. So let's get that cleared up. The main services provided by the Internet are:

E-mail   Send and receive e-mail from anyone on the Internet. Attach files to those messages as well.

World Wide Web (a.k.a., *the Web*, and *www*)   Visit Web pages—those www.*whatever*.com things—go shopping, find information, book a flight, find words that rhyme, get current tax forms, stock quotes, and a whole lot more.

Downloads   There's tons of free stuff you can download (copy) from the Internet to your PC. Both the Web and a service named FTP provide downloading.

Chat   Meet with people from around the world who share similar interests and "chat" live by typing messages back and forth.

Newsgroups (a.k.a., *Usenet*)   Participate in ongoing discussions of any topic that interests you. Also a great place for getting quick, free answers to burning questions on *any* topic.

That may seem like a lot to learn. However, once you've connected to the Internet, you'll be able to learn how to use each service in a matter of minutes. Also, you don't need to learn to use all the services, just those that interest you or will be handy in your work.

What You Need to Connect

To use the Internet, you need three things:

▶ A computer

▶ An account with an Internet Service Provider (ISP)

▶ A *modem* of some sort

Let me quickly review each item. You really need a PC or some kind of computer to use the Internet effectively. You can get *some*

Internet access through alternatives such as WebTV, which is basically a little box that connects to your TV. However, that kind of connection doesn't give you the same range of options that a PC will. As discussed in the Introduction to this book, I'll assume you have a PC and some experience in using it.

Secondly, you'll need to set up an account with an Internet Service Provider (ISP). An ISP is a company or business that has an expensive, high-speed, full-time connection to the Internet. The ISP earns money by offering less expensive *dial-up service* to individuals and small businesses that need access to the Internet. If you haven't already chosen an ISP for your Internet needs, Chapter 3 will help you find one and set up an account.

Finally, you need a modem (or similar device), which is a gadget that connects your PC to a phone line or to your cable TV service. Chapter 2 will help you choose a modem.

Ways to Connect

As mentioned, to gain access to the Internet you'll need to set up an account with an ISP, which acts as an intermediary between your PC and the Internet. Figure 1.1 illustrates the relationship between the Internet, your ISP, and you.

FIGURE 1.1: The Internet, and ISP, and you

Most ISPs offer a variety of connection options, largely centered around how fast you want your connection to operate and how much you're willing to pay. Let's take a look at what I mean by "fast," so you can better make a decision about that.

Connection Speed

The biggest complaint that people have about the Internet is that it's too slow. When they go to see the Web site at http://www.whatever.com, it seems to take forever for the page to appear on their screen. The fact of the matter is, the Internet isn't slow at all. It's pretty speedy in fact. If something is slow, it's probably the connection between you and your Internet Service Provider. Let me explain.

Basically, the Internet provides several different ways for computers to transmit files to one another. The file might be an e-mail message, a Web page—whatever—but it's still a file. The bigger the file, the longer it takes to transmit it from one computer to another. Written text, like you're reading now, can be transmitted quickly over the Internet. But *multimedia* files don't move too quickly. By multimedia file, I mean anything other than text—a photograph, video, sound, music, or a large computer program.

Multimedia files are huge, so they take longer to transmit across the net. The *speed* of your Internet connection is, in essence, a measure of how quickly data can be transmitted to your PC; a measure of how long you have to wait for each item you request from the Internet to appear on your screen.

Now let's look at an example. Let's say you want to view a video that's on the Internet. That video happens to be on a computer that's several thousand miles away from you. When you request the video, the Internet's high-speed cabling can get that entire video across the country and to your ISP in a matter of seconds. That's because the Internet *backbone* (main cable) is designed to handle large files as well as small ones.

Once that video gets to your ISP's computer, it then needs to make the trip to your computer. The connection between your PC and your

ISP determines how long that trip will take. If the connection between you and your ISP is a slow one, it might take several minutes (as opposed to seconds) for the video file to make that final leg of its journey. On the other hand, if the connection between your PC and ISP is a fast one, the wait will be much less.

The speed of an Internet connection is measured in kilobits per second (abbreviated *kbs* or just *k*), where a kilobit is about 1,000 bits. Really fast device speeds are expressed in megabits per second (*mbs*), where one megabit is about a million bits. It takes eight bits to make a byte, and one byte to make a character like the letter "a" or the letter "c." It takes thousands, or even millions of bits, to make a color photograph. But all you need to remember is that the higher the "k," or "m," the faster the device. For example, a 56k modem is twice as fast as a 28k modem. Simple.

In the next three sections we'll look at the three most common methods for connecting to the Internet, and I'll discuss how they compare in terms of speed and cost.

NOTE

A generic term for "how much stuff a cable or wire can move" is *bandwidth*. A high-bandwidth cable carries more information faster than a low-bandwidth copper telephone wire.

Phone Dial-Up

Most people access the Internet through a standard dial-up account. This is where you use a regular telephone line and a modem to dial into your Internet Service Provider on an as-needed basis. This type of account is also called a PPP account (which stands for Point-To-Point Protocol). If you're using Windows 95 or Windows 98, your PC already has all the stuff it needs to connect to such an account. In fact, if your modem is all hooked up and ready to go, the Internet Connection Wizard can have you signed up and online in minutes (as long as you have your credit card handy). I'll discuss the Internet Connection Wizard in Chapter 3.

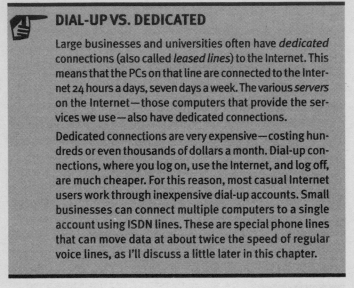

DIAL-UP VS. DEDICATED

Large businesses and universities often have *dedicated* connections (also called *leased lines*) to the Internet. This means that the PCs on that line are connected to the Internet 24 hours a days, seven days a week. The various *servers* on the Internet—those computers that provide the services we use—also have dedicated connections.

Dedicated connections are very expensive—costing hundreds or even thousands of dollars a month. Dial-up connections, where you log on, use the Internet, and log off, are much cheaper. For this reason, most casual Internet users work through inexpensive dial-up accounts. Small businesses can connect multiple computers to a single account using ISDN lines. These are special phone lines that can move data at about twice the speed of regular voice lines, as I'll discuss a little later in this chapter.

If you plan to use a dial-up account to access the Internet, you'll have many ISPs to choose from. The main trick will be finding an ISP that can provide the services you want, along with a dial-up phone number with a prefix that's in your free-calling area. If you can find an access number that you can dial for free, your Internet costs will be limited to whatever you have to pay the ISP. That is, you won't have Ma Bell tacking on long-distance charges every time you connect to the Internet.

TIP

The White Pages of many phone directories include a section listing "Local and Nearby Dialog" numbers that tell you which dialing prefixes you can dial for free. You may want to keep that information handy as you're checking out potential ISPs.

Because most people use the inexpensive, standard dial-up account to access the Internet, Chapters 2 and 3 focus on setting up that kind of a connection.

Cable TV and Satellite Dishes

If you have cable TV or a satellite dish, chances are you already have the best and fastest Internet access available to consumers and small businesses. To get Internet access, you'll need to contact your cable or satellite dish provider. Find out if they have Internet access and how much it costs. These methods aren't the cheapest, but they sure are the fastest!

Find out if your cable or satellite provider offers one-way or two-way access. If it's one-way access, then you'll still need to use your phone to connect to the Internet. If you only have one phone line, anyone trying to call you while you're on the Internet will get a busy signal. You'll also have to disable call-waiting on that line, as that service can disrupt your Internet connection. If that's not acceptable, you'll have to get another phone line, which adds to your costs.

Find out if the provider will come to your location and get the computer(s) connected to the net. If they don't, then there's going to be some do-it-yourself involved. Your provider should be able to give you all the information you need, but it's definitely worth checking out what they offer to do for you. If they set up everything for you and show you how to work it, you'll be able to skip Chapters 2 through 4 and start browsing the Web (Chapter 5) right away.

ISDN Dial-Up

ISDN, which stands for Integrated Services Digital Network, is a special service offered by some phone companies around the country. The advantage to ISDN is that you get two lines, each of which can transmit at 64k, for a total of 128k access. Pretty speedy compared to a 56k modem, but it's not cheap. You first need purchase the ISDN service from your local telephone company. There will be installation charges, as well as a monthly charge. Then you need to find an Internet Service Provider that supports ISDN. The ISDN account might be more expensive than a standard dial-up account, adding even more to the cost of this type of connection.

And, as with regular phone lines, long-distance charges from the phone company still apply if you have to dial outside your own free-dialing range. So you'll want to find an ISP who can offer an ISDN phone number within your free-calling area.

Unfortunately, I can't give you instructions for setting up an ISDN account. How all that works out will depend on your phone company, the equipment they support, as well as the capabilities of your ISP. Hence, you should ignore Chapter 2 in this book. It applies only to standard modems. When looking for an ISP in Chapter 3, you'll need to limit yourself to those that support ISDN connections.

INTRANETS AND EXTRANETS

If you work in a corporate environment, you might hear of *intranets* and *extranets*. An *intranet* is a local area network (LAN) which connects several computers within a business. That smaller network is designed to work just like the larger Internet and allows workers in that environment to use their small local network, as well as the larger global Internet, with one set of skills.

An extranet is also a smaller network that looks and acts like the larger global Internet. However, an extranet is generally used to connect the computers of two or more businesses that are involved in some kind of electronic commerce or some other business-to-business relationship. It may also allow customers outside the company to access resources within the company. Either way, the basic idea is the same: It allows people to use their Internet skills to access the resources of a specific company or groups of companies.

The Worst Comes First

Using the Internet is really easy. Unfortunately, the hardest stuff to learn comes first. All the different ways you can get connected and the wide array of services to choose from makes it all seem a bit overwhelming at first. It also makes it difficult for me to give you simple step-by-step instructions for getting connected to the Internet. You may need to get some information and instructions from your selected ISP. But don't worry. Over the next two chapters you'll learn a lot more about the options available to you. Hopefully, by the time you've finished Chapter 3, you'll be hooked up, online, and ready to surf the net.

Good Things to Remember

So much for our crash course on what the Internet is and how you'll connect. Let's take a moment to review the main points made in this chapter. Then we'll move on to Chapter 2, where you'll learn how to set up your modem to access the Internet.

▶ The Internet is a huge network of computers connected by cables throughout the world.

▶ The Internet offers a variety of services including e-mail, the World Wide Web, newsgroups, and chatting.

▶ To get the most from the Internet, you need a PC, an account with an Internet Service Provider (ISP), and a modem or similar device to attach your PC to the phone line or cable.

Chapter 2

CHOOSING AND INSTALLING A MODEM

Many PCs come with a modem already built in. If you're one of those fortunate enough to have such a PC, all you really need to do is connect the Line jack on the back of your PC to the telephone jack on the wall. If you plan to use the same phone number for voice conversations, then you should also connect the Phone jack on the back of the PC to your telephone. Once you do that, you can skip this chapter and go right on to Chapter 3. If you don't already have a modem, or are looking to upgrade to a better, faster modem, then you'll want to read this chapter.

Choosing a Modem

If your PC doesn't have a modem built in, or doesn't have the kind of modem you want to use for your Internet connection, then you'll need to purchase and install a new modem. There are different kinds of modems available for different kinds of connections. For starters, you need to understand the following:

▶ If you'll be connecting to the Internet via a cable TV or satellite provider, you must use whatever modem they supply or recommend. A standard telephone modem won't do.

▶ If you'll be connecting to the Internet via an ISDN line, you'll need an ISDN Terminal Adapter (also called an ISDN modem). Your phone company might recommend, and even install, a specific modem.

If, like most people, you opt to go with a standard modem, then you'll have many products to choose from, each with its own special features. The main things you want to be concerned about though are:

1. The modem's speed (I recommend a 56k, V.90 modem).

2. The modem's compatibility with your PC. For example, if you have Windows 95 or Windows 98, then you'll want a modem that's compatible with Windows 95. (Anything that's compatible with Windows 95 is also compatible with Windows 98).

You can also choose between three basic models:

External modem   A modem that resides outside of your computer and has cables connecting it to your PC and to your phone line.

Internal modem   A modem that's installed inside the PC, leaving only a telephone jack exposed out the back of the computer. If you're not comfortable installing internal devices, the store that sells you the modem can probably install it for you.

PC Card modem   If you plan to access the Internet from your laptop computer, you might want to consider a PC Card modem, which fits into the PCMCIA slot on your laptop computer.

K56FLEX, X2, AND V.90

The 56k modems come in three flavors: x2, K56flex, and V.90. This is dreadfully confusing, but I can simplify matters for you. When shopping for a 56k modem, I suggest you try to find one that supports the V.90 standard, as this is the most recent and the one supported by most ISPs. However, if you already have a K56flex or x2 modem, don't worry about it. Most ISPs that support the V.90 flavor also support the flex and x2 flavors. Also, many K56flex and x2 modem manufacturers offer updates to convert your existing modem to the V.90 standard.

Please don't let all of this confuse you. Like I said, most ISPs support the all flavors of 56k modems and therefore you needn't worry if you don't even know which standard your current modem uses. If you *really* want to learn more about 56k modems and the various standards they support and you have Internet access from school or work, you can point your Web browser to http://www.56k.com to learn more.

If you feel overwhelmed by all the choices available at your local computer store, just ask someone for help. If you really want to make things simple, I suggest taking your PC's system unit (the big boxy part) to your computer store. Have someone there help you pick out an internal 56k V.90 modem—and then have them install it as well.

Installing the Modem

If you purchase a standard modem, you need to install it as per the instructions that came with the modem. If you inherited the modem from someone and have no written instructions for setting it up, the following sections should help you get the modem installed. Notice that there are separate instructions for external, internal, and PC Card modems.

Installing an External Modem

If you bought, borrowed, or stole an external modem, you need to follow these steps to get it connected to your PC:

1. Close all open windows and programs on your PC and then shut down windows (Select Start ➢ Shut Down and then choose the Shut Down option and click OK).

2. When Windows has shut down, turn off the power to your PC.

3. Use a standard telephone cable to connect the Line or TelCo jack on the modem to the phone jack on the wall. If you're missing any cables, you can easily find replacements at just about any computer store.

4. If you plan to use this same phone line for voice conversations, use a standard telephone cable to connect the Phone jack on the modem to your telephone.

5. Use the supplied modem cable to connect the modem to the COM 1 or COM 2 serial port on the back of your computer.

6. Use the power cable that came with your external modem to plug the modem into the wall, just like a lamp.

When you've finished, the arrangement of cables should look something like the diagram shown in Figure 2.1. You can skip to the section titled "Installing Modem Drivers" later in this chapter once all the cables are in place.

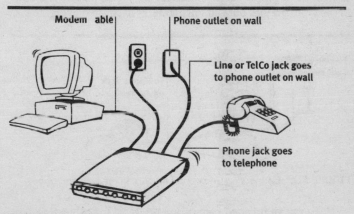

FIGURE 2.1: A typical external modem all hooked up and ready to roll

Installing an Internal Modem

Installing anything inside your computer is risky business for a beginner. If you plan to install an internal modem and have no written instructions for it (and no experience installing cards into the computer), I *strongly* suggest you have it installed professionally. Just about any computer store that offers upgrades could install the modem for you. If you have experience in these matters or have written instructions for installing your internal modem, then you can go ahead and install it yourself.

WARNING

Always shut down Windows, turn off the PC, and unplug it before removing the cover and adding a new card. Failure to do so can ruin your PC!

Once the modem is installed inside the PC, connecting it is easy. You just need two phone cables. Use one cable to connect the Line or TelCo jack on the back of the PC to the phone outlet on the wall. If you plan to use this same phone line for voice communications, use the other phone cable to connect the Phone jack on the back of the PC to the jack on your telephone, as illustrated in Figure 2.2.

FIGURE 2.2: Connecting an internal modem to the wall and phone

When you've finished connecting the cable (or cables), skip to the section titled "Installing Modem Drivers" later in this chapter.

Installing a PC Card Modem

If you have a laptop and it doesn't already have a modem built into it, you can purchase a PC Card modem that fits into the PC Card slot (also known as the PCMCIA slot) of your laptop computer. If your PC supports *hot-swapping*, which allows you to change cards on the fly, you can just plug the modem into the PCMCIA slot, and the cable from that card into the telephone jack on your wall, as illustrated in Figure 2.3.

If your PC doesn't support hot-swapping (or you don't know whether it does or not), no big deal. Just shut down Windows and turn off your computer. Then put the modem into the PCMCIA slot and connect it to the phone jack on the wall. Now you're ready to move onto the next section.

FIGURE 2.3: The PC Card modem goes into PCMCIA slot and connects to phone jack on the wall.

Installing Modem Drivers

Every hardware device (gadget) that you connect to your computer—including your modem—needs to have a special little program called a *driver* (or *device driver*) installed so that the device works properly. You need only install the driver once—not each time you plan to use the modem. To get started, follow these steps:

1. If you're using an external modem, make sure you turn it on first (most external modems have their own on/off switch).

2. Start your computer normally to get to the Windows desktop.

3. If Windows detects your new modem during startup, it will present instructions to help you install the appropriate drivers. Go ahead and follow the instructions as they're presented.

If Windows doesn't detect your new modem, or if you're not so sure whether your modem drivers have been installed, follow the steps below:

1. Make sure your modem is connected properly. If it's an external modem, be sure to turn it on.

2. Starting at the Windows desktop, click the Start button and choose Settings ➤ Control Panel.

3. Within the Control Panel, open the Modems icon.

4. If you see a dialog box titled Modems Properties, then your modem drivers are already installed. You're done! You can move on to Chapter 3 now.

5. If you see a Wizard titled Install New Modem, as shown in Figure 2.4, leave the check box empty, click the Next> button, and follow the instructions that appear on the screen.

Just follow each page of instructions that appears and click the Next> button. Do so until you get to the final Wizard page, which will include a Finish button. After you click that Finish button and respond other instructions on the screen (if any), your modem and its drivers should be fully installed and functional.

ICON? OPEN? HUH?

Like I said in the Introduction to this book, I assume you already know the basics of how to work a PC and Windows. My *Windows 98 To Go* book covers everything you need to know. If you're trying to learn to use the Internet without first learning to use Windows, you have a long tough road ahead of you. While I can't teach you everything about Windows here in an Internet book, I can provide a little assistance as we go along.

To open an icon in Windows 95, you need to double-click it. In Windows 98, you may need to click once or you may need to double-click. It all depends on whether you're using Web (single-click) or Classic (double-click) navigation. To choose one option or the other, click the Windows 98 Start button and choose Settings ➤Folder Options. The navigation options are on the General tab.

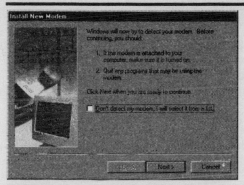

FIGURE 2.4: The Install New Modem Wizard

Troubleshooting Modem Problems

If you have any problems using your modem, refer to Appendix B for help. Also, try the built-in troubleshooters, as discussed under "Troubleshooting Tools" in that same Appendix.

Good Things to Remember

To access the Internet from your PC, you need to get a modem or similar choice and an account with an ISP. This chapter has discussed the different types of modems available to you and general procedures for getting a modem connected and working. Let's review the important points:

▶ Most people use standard telephone lines and modems to connect to the Internet because they're inexpensive and sufficient for casual use.

▶ Many PCs come with modems already built in. To use such a modem, you just need to connect the Line plug on the back of the PC to the telephone jack on the wall. Then, if you plan to use the same phone number for voice conversations, also connect the Phone jack on the back of the PC to the telephone.

▶ If you do need to buy a new modem, try to get a 56k V.90 modem that's compatible with your PC's operating system (e.g., Windows).

▶ If you do buy a new modem, follow the manufacturer's instructions for installing the modem and the modem drivers.

Chapter 3

CHOOSING AN INTERNET SERVICE PROVIDER

With your modem hooked up, it's now time to go hunting for an Internet Service Provider. Keep in mind that if you get an account with one of the leading commercial online services, such as America Online, MSN (the Microsoft Network), CompuServe, or Prodigy, you already have an ISP—that commercial service. Also, if you have a cable or satellite dish connection to the Internet, your cable/satellite provider may very well be your ISP. You'll need to follow the service provider's instructions to access the Internet. There's no reason to read this chapter if you already have access to the Internet through some service.

If you don't have access to the Internet or are looking to switch to a new Internet Service Provider, then read on in this chapter. Here you'll learn about the different factors to consider before choosing an ISP, as well as how to go about finding ISPs. The focus here is on finding ISPs that support standard modem access at speeds up to 56k. However, many of these ISPs also support ISDN access.

Things to Consider

There are quite a few factors to take into consideration before choosing an Internet Service Provider. In the sections that follow, I'll briefly describe the options you need to consider.

Cost

There are lots of ISPs out there vying for your business. And they all know that in order to compete, they need to charge roughly the same as the other guys. You can pretty much figure on spending about $20.00 a month for unlimited Internet access. Some services offer reduced-cost access where you can use the Internet for, say, 150 hours a month for about $7.00 a month. Others offer a free trial period where you can try the service for a while without paying anything.

Keep in mind that in order to avoid Ma Bell's long distance charges, you must find an ISP that can provide a dial-up number within your free dialing area. The white pages of your local tele-phone directory probably includes a "Local and Nearby Dialing" section that tells you which prefixes you can dial for free. Make a note of those prefixes and try to find an ISP that can give you a dial-up number with one of those prefixes. Some services also offer other ways to avoid long-distance charges, such as 800 numbers that you can dial. But there may be a slight additional cost for 800 access.

Modem Support

To take advantage of your modem's top speed, you need to find an ISP that supports that speed. At this writing, 56k is about tops for dial-up modems, and most ISPs support that speed. You might come across ISPs that offer K56flex, x2, and/or V.90 support, but don't let that confuse you. While its true that some 56k modems use one technology or the other, most Internet Service Providers that support 56k modems support all the standards.

Technical Support

Most ISPs offer some type of technical support to help you get over hurdles in setting up your Internet connection. An ISP that offers live telephone technical support 24 hours a day, seven days a week, is the most convenient. ISPs that offer only e-mail support are not as useful because if your connection goes down (or you've never got-ten it up), it's impossible to send and receive e-mail. In the early days of the Internet, it was difficult to find ISPs that provided live technical support. But nowadays, the majority of ISPs offer live sup-port because so many people need a little help from time-to-time (especially when setting up their connection for the first time).

Multiple Dial-Up Regions

If you're a high-tech road warrior and plan to add Internet con-nectivity to your laptop, look for an ISP that can allow you to dial into your account from all around the country without racking up long distance charges. Most of the national ISPs offer this service. For example, AT&T WorldNet offers over 450 phone numbers spread throughout the country. When you're on the road, you can look up a local phone number for the area you're in and then use that number to access the Internet toll-free.

Some ISPs also offer 800 or 888 numbers for dial-up access so you can dial in from anywhere without long distance charges. Be aware, however, that an Internet account that supports 800 number access might cost more than a standard account.

Family Filtering

The uncensored, no-holds-barred rules of the Internet present a dicey situation for parents to deal with. There are many topics and sites on the net that are totally inappropriate for children. Some ISPs offer parental controls that allow parents to set limits on what their children can access. However, if you sign up with an ISP that has no such service, you can still limit kids access to the raunchy stuff via filtering programs and services. For more information, see "Kid-Safe Surfing" in Chapter 7.

Personal Web Space

If you've ever thought of having your own Web page, you'll want to find an ISP that provides free personal Web space. Most ISPs offer 5 or 6 megabytes of personal Web space as part of their service package. Personal Web space assumes that you will not be using the Web site to conduct business. If you're looking to do business on the Web, you'll need more space. But I wouldn't worry about that right away. Before you set up shop on the Web, you'll need a lot of experience in using the Internet and the Web itself.

There's really not enough room in this book to discuss publishing your own Web pages. That's a book-length topic in itself. If you are interested in creating Web pages, the FrontPage Express program, which comes with Microsoft Internet Explorer and Windows 98, is a good candidate for getting started.

Virtual Domain Name, Virtual Hosting

A *domain name* is the last two parts of an e-mail address or Web site's URL. (The URL acronym stands for Uniform Resource Locator, though many people just call it the site's *address*.) For example in www.coolnerds.com and alan@coolnerds.com, the domain name is *coolnerds.com*. Most accounts will only allow you to use their name in e-mail addresses and Web sites. For example, if you sign up with AcmeNet as your Internet Service Provider, your e-mail address might be *yournamehere*@acmenet.com. If that ISP also offers free Web space, your personal Web site's URL might be something like www.acmenet.com/~*yournamehere*.

TIP

By the way, my custom domain name really is coolnerds.com. So once you learn how, you can e-mail me at alan@coolnerds.com and visit my Web site at http://www.coolnerds.com.

If you want your own custom domain name, you'll need to find an Internet Service Provider that offers *virtual hosting*. You'll also need to check (or have your ISP check for you) to see if the domain name you want is available. You may need to think up several possible names, as many names are already taken. If you find an available domain name that you want, you'll need to reserve that name. That'll cost some money. You'll also have to pay an annual fee to keep that name. For exact costs, contact your ISP (or potential ISPs).

Get an Account Right Now

One advantage of going with a national ISP is that you can sign up for an account and then start using the Internet right away. The Windows 95/98 Internet Connection Wizard provides everything you need. Here's how you use it:

1. Grab a credit card. You'll need it to set up an account.

2. Keep handy the list of phone number prefixes that you can dial for free so that you'll pick an appropriate phone number when given your options.

3. Make sure your modem is all hooked up and ready to go. The Internet Connection Wizard can't work without it.

4. If you have any open programs or windows on your Windows desktop, close them.

5. Click the Start button and choose Programs ➤ Internet Explorer ➤ Connection Wizard.

NOTE

If the Internet Connection Wizard isn't available on your PC, it may not have been installed. See "Installing Missing Windows Programs" in Appendix B for help in installing that program.

6. Assuming you're setting up a new account, choose the first option on the first Wizard screen (Figure 3.1) and then click the Next button. The Wizard will connect, via modem, to Microsoft's ISP Referral Service. That might take a couple of minutes.

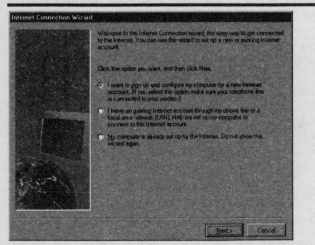

FIGURE 3.1: The first page of the Internet Connection Wizard

7. When the list of ISPs appears (Figure 3.2), you can click any ISP name in the left column to learn more about that ISP's services.

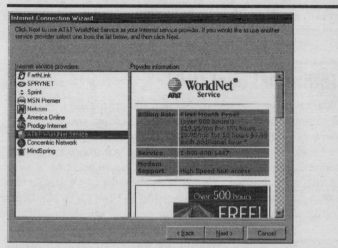

FIGURE 3.2: List of available ISPs in the Internet Connection Wizard

8. After reading through the available services, choose one by clicking it. Then click the Next button to set up an account with the selected service.

9. The exact series of Wizard screens that follows will depend on the service provider you selected. Just follow the instructions and fill in the blanks on each Wizard screen that appears. Then click the Next button to move to the next screen.

NOTE

If at some point you cannot continue with the Wizard—because you don't have enough information, or because they can't provide a phone number that you can dial for free—just click the Cancel button at the bottom of the Wizard screen.

From here on out, you'll need to rely on the Wizard to finish the job. I can't predict the steps you'll need to go through to complete your account with your chosen ISP. However, these ISPs have tried to make getting online as simple as possible, so you shouldn't have any problems. If you do have problems, your best bet would be to contact your selected ISP using the phone number provided by that ISP.

Finding a Local ISP

If you can't find a phone number that you can dial for free among the national ISPs, or you can't find the services you want, consider contacting a local ISP. Most advertise in local papers and Yellow Pages. When you find such a service, you may want to give them a call to learn more about setting up an account. Again, because there are thousands of ISPs around, I can't predict the exact sequence of steps you'll need to go through to set up an account with your selected ISP. But your ISP will (hopefully) be able to tell you exactly what you need to do. Once you have a username (or login name), password, and whatever other information from Table 3.1 that your ISP provides, you can use the Windows Internet Connection Wizard to set up your local account, as discussed next.

Setting Up a Local Account

You can use the Windows 95/98 Internet Connection Wizard to set up your computer to work with a local ISP. You'll first need to set up your account with that ISP and get a username, password, phone number to dial into, and so forth. Once you have that information, here's how you can use the Internet Connection Wizard to set up your account.

1. Click the Windows Start button.

2. Choose Programs ➤Internet Explorer ➤Connection Wizard.

3. Choose the second option, *I have an existing Internet account through my phone line...*

4. Click the Next button.

5. Answer questions and follow the instructions as they appear on the screen.

If you have problems, your best bet would be to contact your ISP. They know best what's needed to get your PC working with the service they provide.

Things to Jot Down

When you do get an Internet account, particularly if you go with a local ISP, you may be bombarded with usernames, passwords, IP addresses, and other weird things that may not seem important at first. However, you may need that information when you first set up your account. Table 3.1 lists the kinds of information your ISP *may* provide and gives examples of what that information will look like. I've left the third column blank so you can fill in your own information when your ISP provides it. Don't worry if you don't get enough information to fill in all the blanks. Some ISPs handle those elements automatically, in which case there's no reason for you to keep track of that information.

WARNING

Usernames, passwords and such are often *case-sensitive*, meaning that when typing the name you have to use the exact upper/lowercase letters provided by your ISP. For instance, the passwords "dipthong" and "Dipthong" are *not* the same when typing a case-sensitive password. So when writing that information into the table and when typing it on our screen, always use the exact upper and lowercase letters provided by your ISP.

TABLE 3.1: Use the third column to fill in information about your account as provided by your ISP.

INFO	EXAMPLE	YOUR ACCOUNT
1. Username/Login name	alan	
2. Login password	whatever	
3. Dial-Up access number	(619)735-8296	
4. Technical support phone	(619)555-1234	
5. Domain name	cts.com	
6. IP address	204.94.78.147	
7. Subnet mask	255.255.255.240	
8. Name Server (DNS) 1	192.188.72.18	
9. Name Server (DNS) 2	192.188.72.21	
10. E-mail address used by people sending you mail	alan@cts.com	
11. Incoming (POP3) mail server	crash.cts.com	
12. Outgoing (SMTP) mail server	smtp.cts.com	
13. E-mail username	alan	
14. E-mail password	whatever	
15. Personal Web space URL	http://www.cts.com/~alan	
16. News (NNTP) server	news2@cts.com	

Good Things to Remember

By the time you've finished reading this chapter, you should have some kind of Internet account set up. Once your account is set up, you can use the next chapter to actually get connected to the Internet. That chapter will also cover some last-minute troubleshooting techniques that you can use to solve any problems that arise. But please keep in mind that in this book, I can only give you general instructions. Your ISP is actually your best resource for working out any last-minute technical snafus that prevent you from logging on. To review the main points covered in this chapter:

- ▶ If you already have an account with America Online, CompuServe, MSN (the Microsoft Network) or Prodigy, you can use that service to access the Internet.

- ▶ If you need to set up a new Internet account and like the convenience of a national ISP, you can use the Windows 95/98 Internet Connection Wizard to set up an account.

- ▶ A local ISP might be better equipped than a national provider to give you a phone number for connecting to the Internet without racking up phone charges.

- ▶ You can learn about ISPs in your area from ads in your local newspaper and Yellow Pages.

Chapter 4

GETTING ONLINE
(AND OFFLINE)

Once you've set up an account with an Internet Service Provider, you're ready to connect to your ISP and start using the Internet. When you're connected to your ISP, your computer is said to be *online*—and you also have access to all the features of the Internet, including the World Wide Web, e-mail, and so forth. The term *offline* means just the opposite of online—you're not connected to your ISP and therefore have no access to the Internet until you go online again.

Let's Do It!

With your Internet account set up, getting online to use the Internet is usually as easy as opening any program that accesses the Internet. For example, most newer versions of Windows come with Microsoft Internet Explorer, a Web browser for viewing pages on the World Wide Web. Once your account is activated, just opening the Internet Explorer program should be sufficient to get you online. Let's give it a whirl:

VOICE MAIL AND MODEMS

Some voice mail systems operate by making a special tone or beep when you first pick up the phone to let you know you have messages waiting. That extra sound (or lack of a dial tone) can confuse a modem and make it malfunction. If you have voice mail, you'd do well to check your messages before you try using the modem. Make sure you can pick up the phone and get a normal dial tone. If *you* get a normal dial tone when you pick up the phone, your modem will also get a normal dial tone when it tries to dial a number.

1. If you have an external modem, make sure it's turned on.

2. Click the Internet Explorer icon on your Windows desktop or click the Windows Start button and choose Programs ➢ Internet Explorer ➢ Internet Explorer.

3. You may see a dialog box like the one in Figure 4.1. (If you *don't* see that dialog box, skip to step 5 now.)

FIGURE 4.1: This dialog box may appear when you first start Microsoft Internet Explorer.

4. Fill in the dialog box as described below:

WARNING

Usernames and passwords can be case-sensitive, which means you must type them using the exact upper and lowercase letters provided by your ISP. Keep this in mind as you fill in the Dial-Up Connection dialog box.

▶ In the User Name test box, type in the username (or login name) provided by your ISP (Item 1 in Table 3.1).

▶ In the Password text box, type in your login password (Item 2 in Table 3.1). It will appear as asterisks to prevent passersby from seeing your password.

▶ If you don't want to have to type your password every time you access the Internet, choose the Save Password option.

▶ If you want your modem to automatically connect to the Internet whenever you start up an Internet program, choose the Connect Automatically option.

▶ Finally, click the Connect button to connect.

5. A dialog box will likely appear on the screen, describing each step it takes as it connects you to your ISP (e.g., "dialing," "verifying username and password").

You may also be prompted to enter your username and password in a small dialog box like the one shown in Figure 4.2. Be sure to type in your username and password (Items 1 and 2 in Table 3.1) using the exact upper and lowercase letters provided by your ISP.

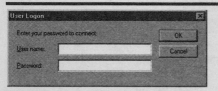

FIGURE 4.2: Sample dialog box requesting username and password for connecting to an Internet account

Once the connection is made and you're online, the dialog box will disappear. A tiny icon, showing two computer monitors, appears in the indicators section of the Windows taskbar, as shown in Figure 4.3. That little indicator tells you that you're now online and ready to use the Internet.

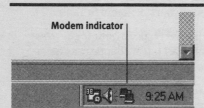

FIGURE 4.3: The online indicator in the Windows taskbar

After the dialog box disappears, your Web browser program will display your default home page. I can't tell you *exactly* what that will look like because pages are subject to changes, making descriptions of them obsolete. But chances are your default home page will be http://www.home.microsoft.com. You'll see the URL in the Address box of your Web browser. The actual page will appear in the larger window, as illustrated in Figure 4.4.

Be aware that it might take a couple of minutes (or more) for the entire page to be loaded into your Web browser. Also, the page may not work correctly if you try to use it before it's been fully downloaded to your PC. You'll know that a page has been completely downloaded to your PC when the status indicator near the lower left corner of Internet Explorer's window shows the word Done.

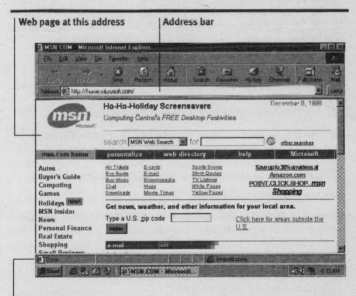

FIGURE 4.4: Microsoft Internet Explorer viewing the page at
http://home.microsoft.com

If you got this far with no snags, you're online. Congratulations! You're now an Internet surfer. Before you start sightseeing though, let me point out just a couple more useful tidbits of information.

NOTE

Remember, if you have trouble getting online, Appendix B and your ISP's technical support will be your best bet for finding solutions.

Another Way to Get Online

Once you have an account with an ISP, opening any Internet-related program on your PC should automatically take you online (if you're not already online). But if that approach doesn't work for you, you can also connect via the Dial-Up Networking program that comes with Windows. Here are the steps to follow:

1. Open My Computer on the Windows desktop.

2. Within My Computer, open the Dial-Up Networking icon.

3. Locate the icon for your Internet connection.

4. Click that icon to open it (or right-click it and choose Connect from the pop-up menu that appears).

5. Click the Connect button in the dialog box that appears.

You'll see a Connecting To... dialog box that keeps you posted on how the connection is going. You may need to enter your username and password (Items 1 and 2 from Table 3.1) and then click the OK button to complete the connection. When the two-monitor icon is visible in the taskbar, you're online and ready to use the Internet. You can start up Microsoft Internet Explorer to start cruising the World Wide Web. You can also use any other service of the Internet simply by starting the appropriate program.

TIP

To make a desktop shortcut to your icon for connecting to the Internet, right-drag the icon out of the Dial-Up Networking folder and onto the desktop. Then release the right mouse button and choose Create Shortcut(s) Here. From then on you can get online simply by opening that new shortcut icon on the desktop.

Logging Off

Remember that whenever you're online, your modem has control of the phone. That means anyone calling you will get a busy signal. Also, if you were unable to find a dial-up number that you can call for free, you'll be racking up your phone bill whenever you're connected to your ISP.

Normally, when you shut down a program that gives you access to the Internet, the connection between you and your ISP will also be shut down. However, you should get in the habit of paying close attention to when you are, and are not, online. Knowing this is simple:

▶ When the modem indicator is visible in the taskbar, you're online.

▶ When the modem indicator isn't visible, you're offline.

If you ever need to go offline manually, just follow these two simple steps:

1. Right-click the modem indicator in the Windows taskbar to reveal its shortcut menu as below.

2. Choose (click) the Disconnect option.

As an alternative to the above, you can just double-click the modem indicator and choose Disconnect from the dialog box that appears. As soon as the modem indicator disappears from the taskbar, you're offline and your telephone line is freed up for normal conversations.

Good Things to Remember

Whew, all this yacking and *still* nothing about using the Internet. Fortunately, this ends the first phase of this book. In the rest of the chapters, I'll assume you have some means of getting online, and therefore focus on the Internet itself. First, a quick review of topics covered in this chapter:

▶ Once your modem is installed and you've set up an account with an ISP, you should be able to get online simply by opening any Internet-related program, such as Microsoft Internet Explorer.

▶ You can also go online by opening Dial-Up Networking and then clicking (or double-clicking in Classic windows navigation style) the icon for the connectoid.

▶ When you're online, a tiny modem indicator (two monitors) is visible in the Windows taskbar.

▶ When you close your Internet-related program, chances are you'll also be taken offline automatically.

▶ If you need to go offline immediately, just double-click the modem indicator in the taskbar or right-click that indicator and choose Disconnect.

Chapter 5

BROWSING THE
WORLD WIDE WEB

The World Wide Web (or just *Web*, for short) is one of the most popular services on the Internet. The Web is the one that has pages for all those www.*whatever*.com addresses you see in ads and such. It's the place to go for information, shopping, weather, news, and more.

The program you use to browse the Web is called a *Web browser*. There are several Web browsers to choose from, including Microsoft Internet Explorer and Netscape Navigator. In this book we'll focus on Internet Explorer, version 4, because it comes with Windows 95 and 98 (therefore I'm just going to go ahead and assume you already have it). If you have some other Web browser, don't worry about it. Later in this chapter I'll show you where you can pick up a free copy of Internet Explorer 4.

Web Buzzwords

Before we start our foray into the Web, I need to define some of the buzzwords that *webheads* (people who are really into the Web) use. For starters, each place that you can visit on the Web is called a *Web site*. There are millions of Web sites out there. Each Web site has its own unique *URL* (Uniform Resource Locator), which is sort of like the site's address or phone number. URLs for Web sites follow the general format:

    www.*wherever*.dom

or

    http://www.*wherever*.dom

The http:// part is optional. Leaving that part out will not cause ill effects in most Web browsers. The www part, as you may have guessed, stands for World Wide Web.

The next part of the URL, where the example shows *wherever*.dom, is the site's *domain name*. Each site has its own unique domain name. The suffix of the domain name tells you what type of organization owns the site, as listed in Table 5.1.

TABLE 5.1: Domain name suffixes

DOMAIN SUFFIX	TYPE	EXAMPLE
.com	Commercial	http://www.toysrus.com
.edu	Education	http://www.ucla.edu
.gov	Government	http://www.cia.gov
.mil	Military	http://www.navy.mil
.net	Large network	http://www.ibm.net

When you first visit a site, you come to that site's *home page*. There may be many other pages within that site, however. Typically you can use *hyperlinks* on the home page to visit other pages within that site. I'll discuss hyperlinks in some detail a little later in this chapter.

A couple of other buzzwords are *client* and *server*. A server is a computer that's connected to the Internet and waits for people to request stuff. Usually, there's nobody sitting at that computer. The computer is pre-programmed to automatically serve up stuff to *clients*. A *Web server* is just a server that's geared toward serving up Web pages via the Internet.

A client, as you may have figured out by now, is any person, program, or computer that requests information from a server. For example, let's say you visit my Web page at http://www.coolnerds .com. In that scenario, you are the client. The Web server is the computer at the domain named coolnerds.com.

Now that you've had your mega-dose of Web jargon, let's talk about your Web browser, the program you use to visit sites on the World Wide Web.

Getting to Know Your Browser

Before we get into the specifics of browsing the Web, let's take a look at Microsoft Internet Explorer, version 4. To start Internet Explorer, use one of the following methods:

▶ Click the Internet Explorer icon on your Windows desktop.

▶ Click the Launch Internet Explorer Browser button in the Windows 98 Quick Launch toolbar.

▶ Click the Start button and choose Programs ➤ Internet Explorer ➤ Internet Explorer.

Microsoft Internet Explorer will start and probably take you to your default home page. But let's take a look at Internet Explorer when it's not displaying a Web page, as shown in Figure 5.1.

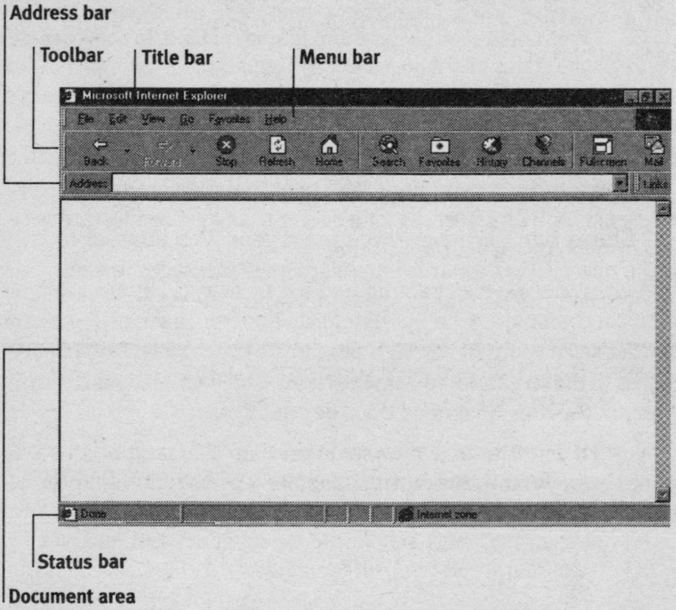

FIGURE 5.1: Microsoft Internet Explorer, Version 4

Title bar   Displays the title of the page you're viewing at that moment (if any) and also holds the standard Maximize, Minimize, and Close buttons.

Menu bar   Plays the same role it does in all programs; just click any menu item to view its pull-down menu.

Toolbar   Contains navigation buttons, Explorer bar buttons, and other hand tools described later in this chapter.

Address bar   Shows the URL (address—the www.whatever.com thing) of the page you're viewing. Also allows you to visit other pages.

> **NOTE**
> If your copy of Microsoft Internet Explorer is missing any of the bars shown in Figure 5.1, you can easily display that bar. Just choose View ➤ Toolbars from Internet Explorer's menu bar and then choose the bar you want to show or hide. To show or hide the status bar, choose View ➤ Status Bar.

Document area   When you view a Web page, it will appear in the document area. That area is blank in Figure 5.1 because I'm not viewing a Web page in that example.

Status bar   Whenever you point your Web browser to a new URL, the status bar will display messages to keep you informed of its progress in loading the page.

> **WHAT IF I DON'T HAVE INTERNET EXPLORER 4?**
>
> If you use some browser other than Microsoft Internet Explorer 4, the instructions presented in this chapter might not exactly match your current browser. In that case, your best bet would be to download Internet Explorer 4 and try it out (don't worry, it's free).
>
> CONTINUED ➡

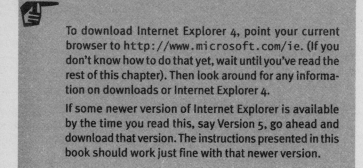

To download Internet Explorer 4, point your current browser to http://www.microsoft.com/ie. (If you don't know how to do that yet, wait until you've read the rest of this chapter). Then look around for any information on downloads or Internet Explorer 4.

If some newer version of Internet Explorer is available by the time you read this, say Version 5, go ahead and download that version. The instructions presented in this book should work just fine with that newer version.

Internet Explorer appears within a standard Windows window, so you can do all the usual things to size and position that window. For example to maximize the window's size, double-click its title bar or click the Maximize button near the upper right corner of the window. To restore a maximized window to a smaller size, double-click the title bar or click the Restore button. To move the window (assuming it isn't maximized), drag the window by its title bar. To size the window (again, assuming it isn't maximized), drag any window border or the sizing pad in the lower right corner of the window.

Fullscreen vs. Windowed View

You can use Microsoft Internet Explorer in either of two different views. You can use the normal windowed view, shown in most figures in this book, or you can use fullscreen view, where only the toolbar appears across the top of the screen and the Web page you're viewing fills the rest. To switch between windowed view and fullscreen view, use one of the following methods:

▶ Choose View ➤ Fullscreen from Internet Explorer's menu bar.

▶ Press the F11 key.

To see the difference between the two views, try pressing the F11 key a few times while Internet Explorer is open and visible on your screen.

Your Default Home Page

Chances are, when you first start your Web browser, its document area won't be blank for long. Instead, when you open your browser, it will connect to the Internet and then display your *default home page*. That page is simply the one that your browser connects to automatically when not given a specific URL to go to. Your default home page is probably `http://home.microsoft.com`, though you can change that at any time, as you'll learn later in this chapter.

Going to a Specific Site

If you already know a Web site's URL, you can visit that site by following these simple steps:

1. Click the URL that's currently in the Address bar to select it, as shown below.

2. Type in the new URL, as shown below.

3. Press the Enter key on your keyboard.

4. Wait—the status bar will keep you posted.

Depending on the speed of your connection, it might take a minute or more for the home page of the site you're visiting to appear. When it does, it will replace whatever page is currently showing in the document area of your Web browser. The word *Done* will appear near the lower left corner of Internet Explorer's window when the entire page has been downloaded.

TIP

If you don't know a particular site's URL, a good first guess is www.*businessname*.com (exclude blank spaces and punctuation marks). For example, www.sears.com, www.charlesschwab.com, www.nytimes.com, www.marthastewart.com, and www.mcdonalds.com are all valid URLs for well-known businesses. Replace .com with .gov for government organizations (e.g., www.nasa.gov) or .edu for schools (e.g., www.harvard.edu). You can also search the Web for particular topics and sites, as I'll discuss in Chapter 6.

Typing-Savers

As an alternative to typing in the entire URL, you can use standard Windows text-editing techniques to change the current URL to some new URL. For example, suppose the address bar is currently pointing to the Web site address http://www.coolnerds.com and you want to visit http://www.yahoo.com. Since both URLs start with http://www and end with .com, you could just change the coolnerds to yahoo, like this:

1. Select the part you want to change by dragging the mouse pointer through it. Below, I've dragged the mouse pointer through coolnerds to select that word.

2. Type in the new word. The new text instantly replaces the selected stuff, as shown below.

3. Press the Enter key on your keyboard.

TIP

If you don't have a specific site that you want to visit right now, try visiting the sites listed in the third column of Table 5.1 (or stop by my site at www.coolnerds.com).

Auto-Complete

Internet Explorer keeps track of the URL of every Web page you visit. When you start typing in a new URL that looks like one you've typed in the past, Internet Explorer automatically fills in the rest of the URL. For example, let's say you've visited http://www.coolnerds.com some time in the past. At the moment, though, you're viewing another Web site. To return to coolnerds, you could just start typing the word *coolnerds* in the Address bar. If you keep your eye on the Address bar as you type, you'll see Internet Explorer expand what you've typed so far into a complete URL, http://www.coolnerds.com in this example.

If and when Internet Explorer shows the complete URL you were intending to type, there's no need for you to keep on typing. Just press Enter to accept the URL that Internet Explorer filled in for you. Occasionally, Internet Explorer will guess wrong and fill in some URL other than the one you intended to type. Not to worry: Just keep typing whatever you intended to type.

Following Hyperlinks

As mentioned, when you visit a Web site you're taken to that site's home page. That page will probably contain *hyperlinks*, more commonly called *links*. A link is any *hot spot* on the page that you can click to go to some other Web site or page. Links in text are often blue and underlined. However, pictures can be links too. If you're not sure whether something on a page is a link, just rest your mouse pointer on the item. If the mouse pointer changes to a little pointing hand, as in any of the examples below, then the item is indeed a hot spot. You can click that spot to make something happen. Depending on the speed of your connection, it might take a minute or more to get to the new page. Watch the status bar for progress.

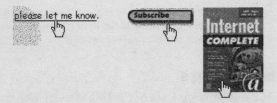

☞ LENGTHY PAGES AND SCREEN AREA

Some pages may be too long to fit on your screen. If a page is larger than what your screen can show, a scroll bar appears at the right edge of your Web browser. You can use the scroll bar, or the Page Up and Page Down keys, to scroll up and down through the page. If your mouse has a wheel on it, you can also scroll up and down using the wheel.

Be aware that many Web designers assume your screen resolution is set to 800 x 600, and their pages look best when displayed at that resolution. To check, and possibly change, your screen resolution, right-click the Windows 95/98 desktop and choose Properties from the menu that appears. Click the Settings tab and adjust the Screen Area slider to *800 by 600 pixels*. Then click the OK button.

CONTINUED ➡

To rearrange your desktop icons after changing your screen area, right-click the Windows desktop again, but this time choose Arrange Icons ➤ By Name.

Navigating Through Visited Sites

Several buttons in Internet Explorer's toolbar, shown below, help you navigate through recently visited sites.

Back   Takes you back to the page you visited before the one you are currently on (if there is one).

Forward   Takes you to the page you just backed out of (again, if there is one).

Stop   If it's taking too long for a page to appear on your screen, you can click the Stop button to stop the transfer. You can then navigate to some other page.

Refresh   Reloads the page from the Web server, ensuring that you have the absolute latest copy of the page.

Home   Takes you back to your default home page.

You may notice that when you revisit a page, it shows up on your screen a lot faster. That's because every time you view a page, Internet Explorer actually downloads (copies) the page from its Web server onto your computer. The files are stored in a folder called the *Internet cache*.

When you revisit a page, Internet Explorer just pulls the copy of that page out of the Internet cache, which is a heck of a lot faster than pulling it over the Internet again. The only downside to this approach is that if the original page on the Web server has changed since your last visit, the page that appears on your screen won't be up to date. But if you click the Refresh button, Internet Explorer will reload the page from the Internet again, even if there is a copy of the page in the cache already.

Using the History Explorer Bar

Internet Explorer also keeps track of sites you've visited in its *history lists*. The Address bar itself contains a short history list, which you can view by clicking the down-pointing arrow at the right edge of the Address bar, as shown below. To revisit any site listed there, just click the site's URL.

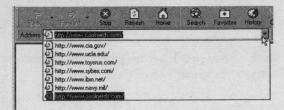

Internet Explorer also maintains a more complete history list, which you can view in Internet Explorer's Explorer Bar. To view that larger history list, do either of the following:

▶ Click the History button in the toolbar.

▶ Choose View ➤ Explorer Bar ➤ History.

The History Explorer Bar opens on the left edge of the screen, as shown in Figure 5.2. Each horizontal bar with the calendar icon in it represents a particular browsing day. If you're just getting started, Today will be the only day listed in your History bar. As time goes by, additional days will be added to the list.

To expand or contract a day, just click it. When the day is open, sites that you visited that day appear in a list. For example, you can see in Figure 5.2 that so far today I've visited the CIA, Coolnerds, IBM, the Navy, Sybex, Toys R Us, and UCLA. Clicking on a particular Web site's folder expands that folder to show specific pages within that site. To revisit a site, just click it in the History bar.

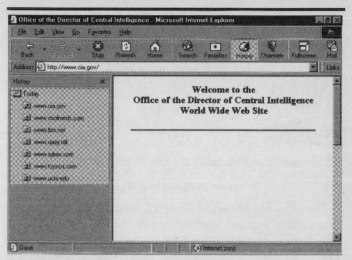

FIGURE 5.2: The History list in the Explorer Bar

TIP
If you share your computer and don't want other people seeing where you've been on the Web, you can remove any URL from the list by right-clicking it and choosing Delete. Optionally, you can clear the entire history list, erasing all traces of where you've been. To empty the History list, choose Tools ➢ Internet Options from Internet Explorer's menu bar. In the dialog box that appears, click the Clear History button and then click the OK button.

You can change the width of the History bar by dragging its right-hand border to the left or right. To close the History bar, click the Close (X) button at the top of the bar.

Changing Your Default Home Page

As mentioned, your default home page is the one that your Web browser goes to automatically when you first open it up. Typically that will be `http://home.microsoft.com` if you're using Microsoft Internet Explorer. To choose some other Web site as your default home page, follow these simple steps:

1. Browse to whatever page you want to make your default home page.

2. When the page is fully visible in your Web browser, choose View ➤ Internet Options from Internet Explorer's menu bar.

3. Under Home Page, click the Use Current button.

4. Click the OK button near the bottom of the dialog box.

The dialog box closes and not much seems to happen. However, the next time you open your Web browser from the Windows desktop, it will go straight to the page you've chosen as your default home page. Clicking the Home button in Internet Explorer's toolbar will also take you directly to that page.

Ending Your Browsing Session

When you're done browsing for the time being, you can end your session by closing your Internet Explorer program. You can use either of the following methods:

▶ Click the Close (X) button in the upper right corner of Internet Explorer's window.

▶ Choose File ➤ Exit from Internet Explorer's menu bar.

Most likely, Windows will disconnect you from the Internet when you close Internet Explorer, thereby freeing up your phone line again. If you want to make sure you are offline, just take a peek at the right edge of the Windows taskbar to see if the two-monitor icon is there. If it still is, you can right-click it and choose Disconnect to make sure you're no longer online.

Good Things to Remember

Surprisingly, what we've covered in this chapter represents about 90% of what you really need to know to browse the Web. In the next chapter, you'll learn how to locate, and keep track of, specific types of information. First, let's take a moment to review the main topics discussed in this chapter:

▶ To browse the World Wide Web, just open your Microsoft Internet Explorer program.

▶ The first page you come to after opening your Web browser is your default home page.

▶ To visit some other site on the Web, type its URL into Internet Explorer's Address bar and then press Enter.

▶ If you don't know a particular business' URL, a good guess is www.*businessname*.com.

▶ Most pages contain hyperlinks (hot spots) that take you to other pages. To follow a hyperlink, just click it.

▶ The Back, Forward, Home, Stop, and Refresh buttons in Internet Explorer's menu bar help you navigate through pages you've visited during your current browsing session.

▶ The History bar keeps track of all URLs you've visited. To view the History bar, click the History button in Internet Explorer's toolbar.

Chapter 6

Search and Seizure (Finding and Downloading)

T here are millions of pages on the Web. If you just browse around at random, you may come across pages that interest you from time to time. However, you can also search the entire Web for specific topics that interest you. The Web is also home to lots of stuff you can download to your computer and play with for free. In this chapter you'll learn how to search for specific types of pages and how to download things to your PC.

Using Search Engines

A search engine is a computer that regularly goes out and visits the Web, creating an index of pages it finds. It organizes its findings by keywords, so you can easily find pages that relate to a given topic. Some of the more popular search engines and their URLs are given in Table 6.1.

TABLE 6.1: Some popular search engines and their URLs

SEARCH ENGINE	URL
AltaVista	www.altavista.digital.com
AOL NetFind	www.aol.com/netfind
Coolnerds Search*	www.coolnerds.com/search
Excite	www.excite.com
GoTo	www.goto.com
HotBot	www.hotbot.com
Infoseek	www.infoseek.com
LookSmart	www.looksmart.com
Lycos	www.lycos.com
MSN Web Search*	www.msn.com
NetGuide	www.netguide.com
Snap	www.snap.com
WebCrawler	www.webcrawler.com
Yahoo	www.yahoo.com

* Provides access to multiple search engines from a single page.

Most search engines don't censor material, so a search for a seemingly harmless word or phrase could result in a few links to Web sites that contain content that is inappropriate for children. Fortunately, there are some search engines out there that do filter out the raunchy stuff. Table 6.2 lists some of the more popular kid-safe search engines out there.

TABLE 6.2: Search engines for kids, with their URLs

SEARCH ENGINE	URL
AOL NetFind for Kids	www.aol.com/netfind/kids
Disney's Internet Guide	www.disney.go.com/dig/today
Jumbo! For Kids	www.jumbo.com/pages/kids
WebCrawler for Kids	www.webcrawler.com/ctw
Yahooligans	www.yahooligans.com

You can visit a search engine as you would any other site: simply by typing its URL into Internet Explorer's Address bar and pressing Enter. When you get to the site, you'll probably see lots of ads and links. The main thing you'll be looking for is a text box that lets you type in some text and a button for performing the search. The button will probably be labeled *Search* or *Find* or *Go*. But whatever it's labeled it will be very near the textbox, as in the example below.

To use the search engine, type a *search string* (any word or phrase) into that text box. (If the blinking cursor isn't already in that box, click the box first and then start typing.) For example, below I've opted to search for *free stuff.* After typing your search string, click the Search button (or equivalent button) and wait a few seconds.

free stuff| ··············· Search

A long list of sites will appear, as in the example shown in Figure 6.1. You'll probably need to use the scroll bar at the right edge of the Internet Explorer's window to scroll through the entire list. To visit any listed site, just click the underlined hyperlink text.

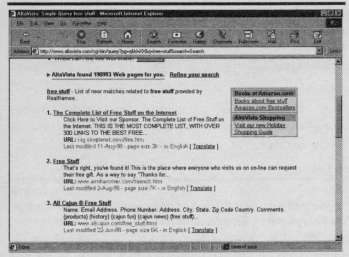

FIGURE 6.1: Results of searching AltaVista for "Free Stuff"

After visiting a page, click the Back button in your Web browser to return to the list of URLs.

TIP

Here's a quick-and-easy shortcut to MSN's search engine. Click the Windows Start button and choose Find ➢ On The Internet.

Searching with the Explorer Bar

As an alternative to visiting an individual search engine, you can use Internet Explorer's Search Explorer Bar to gain quick access

to a few of the more popular search engines. To open the Explorer
Bar, use either of the following methods:

► Click the Search button in Internet Explorer's toolbar.

► Choose View ➤ Explorer Bar ➤ Search.

NOTE
The first time you use the Search Explorer Bar, you may be
asked for permission to download a special program. There's
nothing to worry about—go ahead and perform the download.

The Explorer bar opens at the left edge of the screen, displaying a text box for typing and a Search (or similar) button to start
the search. As usual, you can widen or narrow that bar by dragging left or right the vertical line that separates the Explorer Bar
from the main page.

To choose a specific search engine, click the Choose A Search
Engine button near the top of the Explorer Bar, as shown below.
Then click the engine you want to try.

Search   ×
Choose a Search Engine ▾
AltaVista
GoTo
Infoseek
Lycos
MSN Web Search
AOL NetFind
List of all Search Engines...

A small page for that search engine will eventually appear within
the Explorer bar. Type your search string into the text box that
appears and then click the Search (or similar) button. A list of sites

matching the word or phrase you're searching for appears in the main document window to the right of the Explorer Bar. As usual, you can click any link in that listing to visit the corresponding Web site.

When you've finished using the Search Explorer Bar, you can just click the Close (X) button near the top of the bar to close it.

Advanced Searching

Some searches will yield thousands, if not millions, of sites to visit. Often, you can narrow things down by being more specific in your search string. For example, instead of searching for "free stuff," you could search for "free Windows programs" to narrow the search to just Windows programs.

Be aware, however, that not all search engines will narrow things down using this approach. Some will list sites that contain any word in your search string. For example, a search for "free Windows programs" might list all sites that contain the word "free," all sites that contain the name "Windows," and all sites that contain the word "programs," yielding hundreds of thousands of links.

To narrow the search to sites that contain all the words in your search string, enclose the string in quotation marks or use a plus sign between the words (for example, you would type **"free Windows programs"** or **free+Windows+programs**).

To learn more about a particular search engine's options for refining your searches, go to that site and look around for an "Advanced Search," "Search Tips," or "Help" link. Following that link will generally take you to a page that describes the full range of searching abilities that particular engine offers. With just a little practice, you should be able to find information on just about any topic imaginable.

Downloading Stuff

The Web is home to thousands of freeware and shareware programs. Freeware programs are ones you can just download (copy to your PC) for free. Shareware programs are generally trial versions of programs that you can use for free for a limited time to help you decide whether you want to buy the program. Table 6.3 lists some Web sites that offer both freeware and shareware. As always, you can visit any site by typing its URL into Internet Explorer's menu bar and pressing the Enter key.

TABLE 6.3: Web sites that offer lots of downloads

DOWNLOAD SITE	URL
Download.com	www.download.com
Download.net	www.download.net
Five-Star Shareware	www.5star-shareware.com
Happy Puppy	www.happypuppy.com
Microsoft	www.microsoft.com /msdownload
Pass the Shareware	www.passtheshareware.com
Rocket Download	www.rocketdownload.com
Shareware & Freeware Fonts	http://desktoppublishing.com/fonts-free.html
Shareware Palace	www.sharewareplace.com
Shareware.com	www.shareware.com
SoftSeek	http://mdonline.softseek.com
Software USA	www.softusa.com
The Shareware Net	www.theshareware.net
Tucows	www.tucows.com
Windex	www.windex.daci.net
Wugnet	www.wugnet.com
Ziff-Davis	www.zdnet.com/swlib

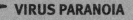

VIRUS PARANOIA

People occasionally plant *viruses*—tiny programs that do bad things to your computer—in programs that people download from the Internet. These viruses are rare and nothing to lose sleep over. The endless virus warnings that pop up on your screen are there partly for legal reasons. Microsoft doesn't want to be held responsible if, while using Microsoft Internet Explorer, you inadvertently download some virus from "Bob's Bargain Basement Software."

If you download from the Web sites of reputable businesses and properly maintained download sites like those listed in Table 6.3, it's very unlikely that your computer will ever catch a virus. Then again, as the saying goes, an ounce of prevention is worth a ton of cure. To protect your PC from catching a virus, consider installing some anti-virus software. For more information, refer to "Anti-Virus Programs" in Appendix A.

When you get to a site that offers downloads, the hotspot that starts a download will look like a hyperlink. But when you click the link, you won't be taken to a new page. Instead, the File Download dialog box, shown in Figure 6.2, will appear, asking what you want to do with the file.

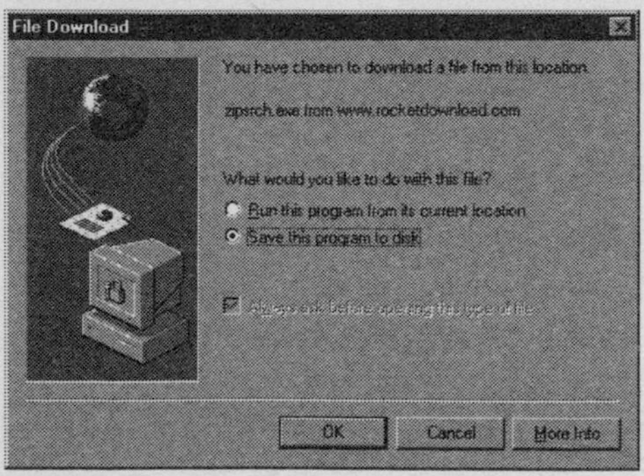

FIGURE 6.2: The File Download dialog box

Typically, you'll want to choose *Save this program to disk* and then click the OK button. This brings up the Save As dialog box, which asks where on your hard drive you want to put the downloaded program. The first thing you want to do is choose which folder to put the downloaded file into. If you can't decide right off the bat, you can just choose Desktop from the top of the Save In drop-down list, as shown below. That way, the icon for the downloaded file will be plainly visible on your Windows desktop as soon as the download is finished.

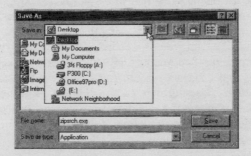

Next, take a look at the name of the file being downloaded, again so you can find it later. That information appears in the File Name text box down lower in the dialog box. For example, in the Save As dialog box shown in the example, the file being downloaded is named `zipsrch.exe`. Finally, click the Save button to begin the download.

A new dialog box, like the one below, will keep you informed of how the download is going. You needn't wait for the download to finish before doing other things: You can work on other stuff. To check on the progress of your download from time to time, just click the File Download button in the Windows taskbar to bring the File Download dialog box back to the screen.

When the download is complete, another dialog box will appear, as shown below.

To use the downloaded file, you typically just have to click its icon. If you put the file in some folder other than the Desktop, you'll need to open that folder first, using the My Computer, Windows Explorer, or Find programs that come with Windows. If you downloaded to the desktop, you just have to close or minimize all open windows to get to the desktop. You should see the icon for the downloaded file somewhere on the desktop, as in the example shown below where the mouse pointer is near the icon for the sample `zipsrch.exe` program I downloaded.

Once downloaded, the file is no different from any other on your PC. Clicking the downloaded file's icon opens that file on your computer. Exactly what happens next depends on the file you downloaded. You'll need to follow the instructions that appear on your screen to use that file.

Zip Files

Many files that you can download are compressed, or *zipped*, to make transfers over the Internet go faster. To open such a file, you'll need a program that's capable of unzipping files. I use a program named WinZip. You can download a shareware version of that program from http://www.winzip.com. Once WinZip is installed on your PC, opening any file that has a ZIP extension on its filename will automatically fire up WinZip. From within the WinZip program, you can just click the Extract button to decompress the downloaded file. For more information on WinZip, see Appendix A.

Adobe PDF Files

Many written documents that you download to your PC will be in Adobe PDF format. To open and read those, you'll need the Adobe Reader program. You can download a free copy of that program from http://www.adobe.com/prodindex/acrobat/readstep.html. The Web page that appears provides complete instructions on downloading and using the reader. Once you've downloaded and installed Adobe reader, clicking (or double-clicking) the icon for any downloaded PDF file will automatically cause that document to appear on your screen in the Adobe reader.

Good Things to Remember

The Web is home to tons of free information and free stuff you can download. Finding information is fairly easy once you learn about the search engines and how to use them. Downloading is easy too, once you find some sites that offer downloads. The main points to remember:

▶ To search the Web for specific information, you can click the Windows Start button and choose Find ➤ On The Internet or go to any search engine listed back in Table 6.1.

▶ When searching for a phrase containing two or more words, enclosing that phrase in quotation marks or putting plus signs (+) between the words, will narrow the search to sites that contain all those words.

▶ To learn the specifics of a given search engine, go to its site and look around for a Help, Advanced Search, or similar link.

▶ Many sites offer files you can download (copy to your PC) for free. Table 6.2 lists some of the more popular download sites.

▶ To start a download, click the link that offers the download. Rather than being taken to a new page, the File Download dialog box appears. Then...

   ▶ In the File Download dialog box, choose *Save this program to disk* and click the OK button.

   ▶ When the Save As dialog box appears, choose a folder to put the downloaded file into. If in doubt, just choose the Desktop folder. Any files placed in that folder will appear on your Windows desktop.

▶ When the download is complete, click (or double-click) the downloaded file's icon to open that file.

Chapter 7

FAVORITES, SUBSCRIPTIONS, AND KID-SAFE SURFING

As you explore the Web, you're likely to come across some pages that you might like to visit again in the future. Microsoft refers to such pages as Favorites and provides tools for organizing and keeping track of them. You can also subscribe to sites to receive notification of when something in the site has changed. This chapter will show you how to track, organize, and subscribe to favorite sites. And lastly, we'll look at the important topic of kid-safe surfing, which is of paramount concern to parents.

Keeping Track of Favorite Sites

If you come across a Web page that you think you'll want to revisit again, you can add that page to your list of favorites. Here's how:

1. While visiting a page that you'd like to add to your favorites, choose Favorites ➢ Add To Favorites from Internet Explorer's menu bar. The dialog box shown below appears.

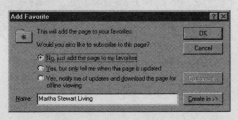

2. To keep things simple, choose the first option, *No, just add the page to my favorites*.

3. Click the OK button.

That's it! To revisit the site in the future, you can just select it from your list of favorites. Here's how:

1. Open Internet Explorer in the usual manner (if it isn't already open).

2. Click Favorites in Internet Explorer's menu bar to open the Favorites menu.

3. The bottom of the menu will contain a list of pages you've added to your favorites, as in the example below. To revisit a site, just click that site's name in the menu.

Simple, eh?

Organizing Your Favorites

As your collection of favorite sites grows, you might want to organize them into categories. For example, you might have a category for favorite search engines, another for favorite download spots, another for favorite shopping sites, and so forth. To do so, you create a folder for each category within the Favorites menu. Here's how:

1. From Internet Explorer's menu bar, choose Favorites ≻ Organize Favorites. The Organize Favorites dialog box shown in Figure 7.1 appears.

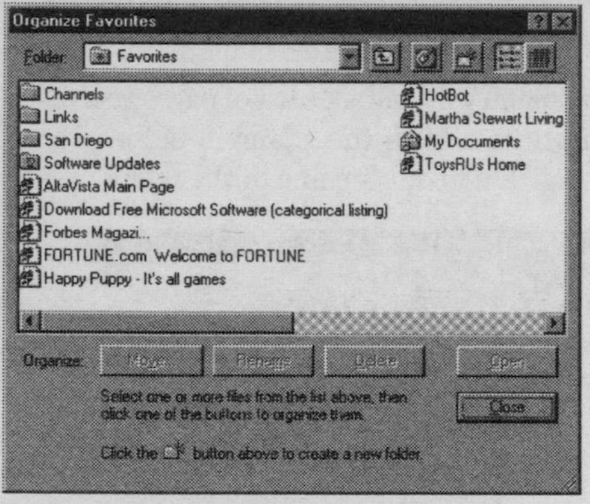

FIGURE 7.1: The Organize Favorites dialog box

2. To create a new folder, click the Create New Folder button in the toolbar (shown below near the mouse pointer). A folder named New Folder appears in the list.

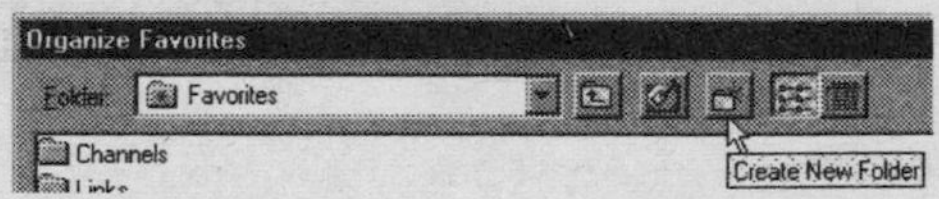

3. Type a new name, of your own choosing, for the folder. Then press Enter.

NOTE

To change the name of a folder after it's been saved, right-click the folder you want to rename, choose Rename from the menu that appears, type the new name, and then press Enter. This approach lets you rename any folder or file on your entire PC.

You can repeat steps 2 and 3 to create as many folders as you like.

Moving Existing Favorites into Folders

Once you've created a folder, you can start moving existing favorites into those folders. Here's how:

1. In the Organize Favorites dialog box, click any site name (not a folder) that you want to move.

2. Click the Move button. The Browse For Folder dialog box shown in Figure 7.2 appears.

FIGURE 7.2:   The Browse For Folders dialog box

3. Click the folder that you want to move the current Favorite into.

4. Click the OK button at the bottom of the Browse For Folders dialog box.

NOTE

If things seem to disappear from your Organize Favorites folder for no reason, don't panic. They may have just scrolled out of view. Use the scroll bars (when available) at the bottom and right of the list to scroll items into view.

The Browse For Folders dialog box closes, and you're returned to the Organize Favorites dialog box. The favorite item you moved will no longer be visible though, because it has been moved into a folder. To see the item, open the folder that you moved the item into by double-clicking the folder name or by clicking the folder name once and then clicking the Open button. The current folder's name appears next to Folder at the top of the Organize Favorites dialog box, and only the contents of the currently open folder are visible.

To return to the parent (Favorites) folder, click the Up One Level button (shown below) in the toolbar. When you've finished organizing your favorites, click the Close button in the Organize Favorites dialog box.

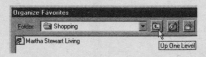

Putting New Favorites into Folders

Once you've added a folder to your favorites, you can easily add new favorites to that folder as you encounter them. For example, let's say you've created a folder named Shopping. You've recently come across a cool site for shopping that you want to add to your favorites—and you want to add this item to the Shopping folder.

First, remember you need to be on the page that you want to add to your favorites. Then, follow these steps:

1. Choose Favorites ➤ Add To Favorites from Internet Explorer's menu bar.

2. In the Add Favorite dialog box that appears, click the Create In >> button to display your list of Favorites folders, as shown in Figure 7.3.

3. Click the Folder you wish to add the favorite item to.

4. Click the OK button near the top of the Add Favorite dialog box.

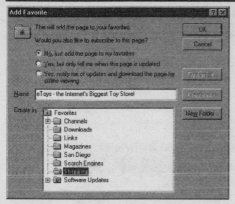

FIGURE 7.3: The Add Favorite dialog box with Favorites folders displayed

The favorite is saved. Now let's take a look at how you revisit favorite sites using your folders.

Using Favorites Folders

Going to favorite sites after organizing them into folders is simply a matter of opening the appropriate folder before you click the site's URL. This just adds one step to the normal procedure for revisiting favorite sites:

1. Click Favorites in Internet Explorer's menu bar. The Favorites menu that opens will include any new folders you've created.

2. Point to (or click) the folder that contains the favorite site you want to revisit. Sites within that folder appear to the right, as shown in Figure 7.4.

3. Click the name of the site you want to visit.

Keep in mind that should you ever decide to reorganize your favorites in the future, you can always return to the Organize Favorites dialog box to create new folders or shuffle things around into different folders.

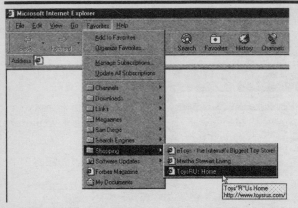

FIGURE 7.4: Favorites within my Shopping folder visible from the Favorites pull-down menu

MAKING DESKTOP SHORTCUTS TO FAVORITE SITES

You can easily create a desktop shortcut icon to any Web page you like. First, browse to the Web page in the usual manner so that it appears in Internet Explorer on your screen. Then, shrink the Internet Explorer window down a little so that you can see some portion of the Windows desktop.

Then, point to the little page icon that appears just to the left of the page's URL in Internet Explorer's Address bar. Drag that little icon out to the Windows desktop and release the mouse button. A larger icon appears on the desktop. You can click that icon at any time in the future to open Internet Explorer and visit the page.

Note that the Organize Favorites dialog box also contains Rename and Delete buttons. You can click any item in the Organize Favorites dialog box and then click the Rename button to change its name or click the Delete button to delete the item. Be aware that when you delete a folder, you also delete all the items within that folder. To avoid doing that, you would first need to open the folder and move any items you want to keep.

The Favorites Explorer Bar

That little Favorites pull-down menu is just one way to access your Favorites. You can also get to them via the Favorites Explorer bar. To open that bar, do either of the following:

▶ Click the Favorites button in Internet Explorer's toolbar.

▶ Choose View ➣ Explorer Bar ➣ Favorites from Internet Explorer's menu bar.

The Favorites explorer bar opens up at the left side of Internet Explorer's window, as shown in Figure 7.5.

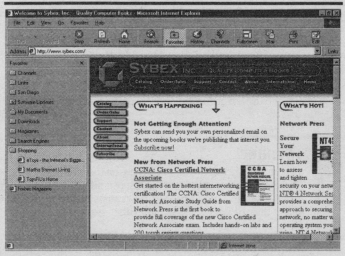

FIGURE 7.5: The Favorites Explorer bar open in Internet Explorer

The Favorites bar contains exactly the same folders and items that the Favorites menu contains. But you work the bar a little differently. To open or close a folder, just click it. When opened, all the sites within that folder are visible. For example, in Figure 7.5, I've already opened the Shopping folder, and you can see the sites listed in that category. To visit a site, just click its name.

As with any Explorer bar, you can adjust the width of the Favorites bar by dragging its right border to the left or right. To close the Favorites bar, just click the Close (X) button near the top of the bar or click the Favorites button in the toolbar again.

TIP

Windows 98 offers yet another quick shortcut to your list of favorites. Click the Windows Start button and point to Favorites on the Start menu that appears.

Understanding Subscriptions

Subscriptions, in Internet Explorer, are yet another means of keeping track of favorite Web sites. Don't let the term "subscription" fool you, though. Unlike magazine subscriptions, Internet Explorer subscriptions don't cost any money, and you needn't worry about getting irritating subscription renewal notices in the mail every week.

WARNING

I don't mean to imply that everything on the Internet is free. There *are* sites out there that sell subscriptions to e-mailed newsletters and such. However, that's something entirely different that the type of subscription discussed in this chapter.

Internet Explorer subscriptions work like this: At about 2:00 A.M. each morning, when you should be in bed, Internet Explorer fires itself up, connects to the Internet, and visits every Web page that you've subscribed to. While visiting the page, it checks the date and time that the page was last modified. Then, it checks the date and time of the corresponding page in your Internet cache. If the two dates and times are the same, then the page hasn't changed since your last visit. So it just goes on to the next subscribed page.

If, however, Internet Explorer discovers that the page on the Web is newer than the page in your Internet cache, then it "knows" that the page has changed since your last visit. In that case, it notifies you that the page has changed by adding a red gleam to the page's icon in your Favorites collection.

That way, the next time you open your Favorites menu or Explorer bar, you can see at a glance what's changed since your last visit, spending your time just checking out the new stuff without wasting time visiting pages that haven't changed since your last visit.

Offline Browsing

Subscriptions also support *offline browsing*, where you can have pages that have changed since your last visit downloaded into your Internet cache. The icons for pages that have changed since your last visit will still be marked with a red gleam. But when you go to visit that page, Internet Explorer need not go online and get the page, because the page has already been put into your Internet cache. Instead, Internet Explorer can read the page right out of your cache, which is much faster than downloading it from the Internet.

The downloading approach is especially handy with laptop computers. You can leave your laptop on during the night and have it download changed pages for you automatically. In the morning, you can disconnect the laptop from the Internet and take it on the subway (or wherever) on your way to work. There, you can browse all the changed pages without even being connected to the Internet, because those changed pages are already in your computer's Internet cache.

Subscribing to a Favorite Site

You can subscribe to *any* Web site using Internet Explorer. The procedure for doing so is almost identical to adding a site to your favorites. Here are the steps:

1. When you're visiting a page that you'd like to subscribe to, choose Favorites ➢ Add To Favorites from Internet Explorer's menu bar.

2. In the Add Favorite dialog box that appears (shown below), choose the second option if you simply want *notification* (where the site's icon in Favorites is marked with a gleam when the page has been changed.) Alternatively, if you want notification *and* the page to be downloaded to your Internet cache, choose the third option.

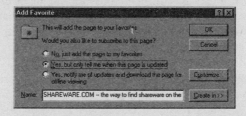

3. If you want to add this favorite to one of your Favorites folders, click the Create In button and choose the folder in which you want to place the favorite.

4. Click the OK button in the Add Favorite dialog box.

That's all there is to it.

Converting Favorites to Subscriptions

Suppose you have a favorite that you created a while ago and you want to change that favorite to a subscription. Easy. Just follow these steps:

1. Open the Favorites explorer bar in Internet Explorer, as described earlier in this chapter.

2. If the favorite that you want to change to a subscription is in some folder, open that folder.

3. Right-click the Favorite that you want to change to a subscription and choose Subscribe from the menu that appears. The Subscribe Favorite dialog box shown below appears.

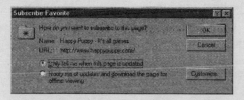

4. If you want notification only (red gleam, no download), choose the first option. If you want notification and downloading, choose the second option.

5. Click the OK button in the Subscribe Favorite dialog box.

Pretty easy, eh? Now that you know *how* to subscribe to Web sites, you need to figure out when, and how often, you want your computer to go out and check the Web for changes. I'll discuss that in the next section.

Scheduling your Subscriptions

The main idea behind subscriptions is to have your PC automatically check for updated pages while you're away from the computer so you can do more constructive things while your at the computer. By default, Internet Explorer checks each site that you've subscribed to at about 2:30 A.M. daily. But you can reschedule that to any time that's convenient for you. You can also have subscriptions checked weekly, monthly, or anywhere in between.

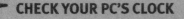

CHECK YOUR PC'S CLOCK

The update schedule will only be accurate if your computer's calendar and clock are accurate. To check and adjust your PC's date and time, double-click the date at the right side of the Windows taskbar or click the Windows Start button and choose Settings ➤ Control Panel. Within the Control Panel, open the Date/Time icon.

In the Date And Time Properties dialog box that appears, set the correct date and time. You can also use the Time Zone tab within that same dialog box to indicate your correct time zone. Click OK to close the dialog box and save your settings when you're done.

Let's suppose, for example, that you work nights and you would prefer to have your daily subscriptions checked at 11:00 A.M. To change the Daily update schedule (or any other schedule for that matter), follow these steps:

1. From Internet Explorer's menu bar, choose Favorites ➤ Manage Subscriptions. The Subscriptions dialog box, shown in Figure 7.6, appears.

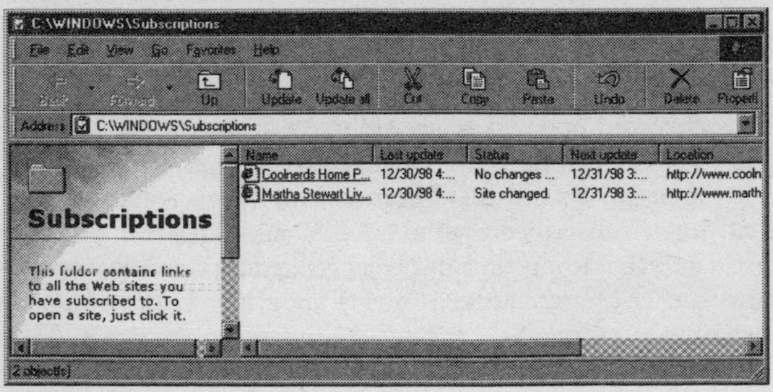

FIGURE 7.6: The Manage Subscriptions dialog box

2. Right-click any site you've subscribed to and then choose Properties from the menu that appears. A dialog box for that subscription appears.

3. Click the Schedule tab to reveal the options shown in Figure 7.7.

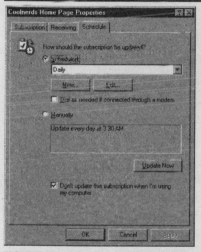

FIGURE 7.7: The Schedule tab of a subscription's Properties dialog box

4. Choose the Scheduled option near the top of the dialog box.

5. Choose Daily (or some other frequency) from the drop-down list under that option.

6. To set a time for *all* Daily subscriptions, click the Edit button. The Custom Schedule dialog box appears.

7. Use the Update At option to determine when daily subscriptions are met. For example, if you look near the mouse pointer in Figure 7.8, you can see I've set the update time to 11:00 A.M.

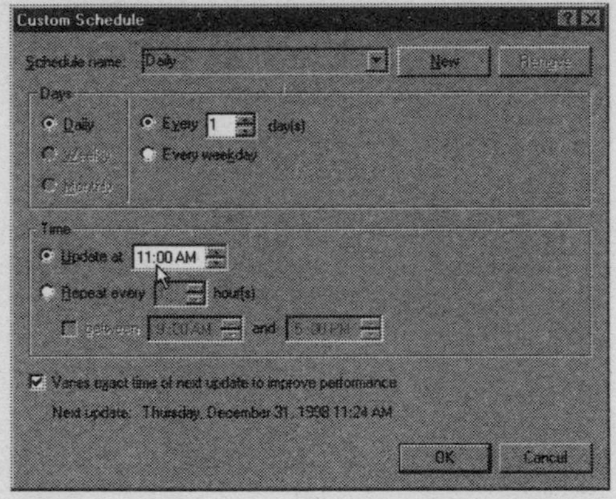

FIGURE 7.8: The Custom Schedule dialog box with daily subscription checking set to take place at 11:00 A.M

8. Click the OK button at the bottom of the Custom Schedule dialog box. Then click the OK button at the bottom of the subscription Properties dialog box.

Be aware that when you change the Daily schedule, *all* subscriptions set to daily updates will be checked at that time. There is no need to go in and set a separate time for each and every subscribed site. What you're really doing is setting the time that the subscription update procedure starts. Once the procedure starts, Internet Explorer will check each and every subscribed site.

Also, it's important that your computer is turned on and running when the schedules time arrives. If you have an external modem, you want to make sure to leave that turned on as well. If either the computer or the modem is shut off when the scheduled time arrives, nothing will happen. You *can* turn off your computer's monitor, printer, and any other devices if you like, to save electricity.

Manually Updating Subscriptions

You can also update your subscriptions manually at any time. This might come in handy if, say, you missed a scheduled update time or you need to know right now which pages have changed since your last visit. To update all your subscriptions in one fell swoop, choose Favorites ➢ Update All Subscriptions from Internet Explorer's menu bar.

How to Browse Offline

If you've opted for notification *and* downloads in your subscriptions and you want to view changed pages offline (without being connected to the Internet), you first need to switch Internet Explorer to offline browsing mode. To do this, from Internet Explorer's menu bar, choose File ➢ Work Offline.

From here on out you'll be limited to browsing pages that have already been downloaded to your Internet cache. The icons for those pages will be marked with the red gleam in your Favorites. So all you need to do is opened any gleamed icon to see the page on your screen.

Note that if you try to browse a page that hasn't been downloaded to your Internet cache, you'll get an error message like the one below. You can choose Stay Offline to keep browsing pages in your Internet cache only or choose Connect to go online. You can also go back to normal online browsing again by choosing File ➢ Work Offline from Internet Explorer's menu bar.

Using Channels

You may have seen the Windows Channel Bar on your desktop at some time (Figure 7.9). Or perhaps you've stumbled across the

Channels Explorer bar and wondered what those items are about.
Actually, channels are just Web sites that use features that only
Microsoft Internet Explorer versions 4 and 5 support.

FIGURE 7.9: The Channel Explorer Bar and desktop Channel Bar

To open the Channel Explorer bar while in Microsoft Internet
Explorer, click the Channels button in Internet Explorer's toolbar
or choose View ➢ Explorer Bar ➢ Channels.

If you have Windows 98, you can follow these steps to view, or
hide, the desktop Channel Bar:

1. Click the Windows 98 Start button and choose Settings ➢
   Active Desktop ➢ Customize My Desktop.

2. On the Web tab select (check) the *View my Active Desktop as a web page* option and Internet Explorer Channel
   Bar options as in Figure 7.10.

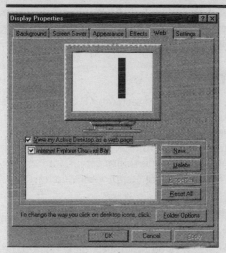

FIGURE 7.10: The Web tab of the Display Properties dialog box

3. Click the OK button near the bottom of the Display Properties dialog box.

The Channel Bar contains several channels already. Some are categorized into groups such as News & Technology, Sports, Business, and so forth. Clicking any group name shows channels within that group. To visit a channel, click its button in either channel bar.

Unlike normal Web sites, most channels open with Internet Explorer in Fullscreen mode. This means that the page will fill your whole screen except for a thin toolbar across the top of the screen. You can easily switch back to the normal view by clicking the Fullscreen button that appears in that toolbar.

To see the full range of currently available channels and to get a better appreciation of what channels are all about, visit the Microsoft Active Channel Guide. Just click its button at the top of the Channel bar and wait a few seconds for the page to load. Exactly what you find there depends on the day you happen to visit. But you shouldn't have any problems getting around, since the channel is really just a Web page with the same kinds of hyperlinks as regular Web pages.

Kid-Safe Surfing

As I've discussed, the Internet is protected by U.S. Freedom of Speech laws, which means pretty much anything goes. While there is plenty of useful information out there on the Web, there are also plenty of sites that are entirely inappropriate for children. For the rest of this chapter, we'll look at specific things parents and schools can do to prevent kids from accessing inappropriate materials.

Internet Explorer Content Ratings

The entertainment industry uses it well-known rating system, G, PG, R, and so forth, to rate movies for age-appropriateness. On the Internet, the Recreational Software Advisory Council (RSACi) plays a similar role. Web sites are rated along four scales: language, nudity, sex, and violence. On each scale the site receives a rating of 0 (none) to 5 (lots). For example, a site with a rating of 0 on the language scale has no foul language. A rating of 5 on the language scale indicates that the site contains foul language of the most offensive kind.

Security settings built into Internet Explorer allow parents to limit access to pages that have been rated by RASCi and also lets parents determine how much of that stuff their child can be exposed to. For example, one parent might feel that their teenager shouldn't see any bad language, in which case they could limit viewing to pages rated 0 on the language scale. Another parent might feel that their teenager can handle a little bad language, allowing sites rated 0 or 1 on the language scale to be viewed.

To set limits on acceptable content in Internet Explorer, follow these steps:

1. Start Microsoft Internet Explorer in the usual manner.

2. Choose View ➤ Internet Options from Internet Explorer's menu bar.

3. Click the Content tab.

4. Under Content Advisor, click the Enable button. The following dialog box appears.

![Create Supervisor Password dialog box]

5. Make up a password and type it into both the top and bottom text boxes. This will be the "supervisor password" that allows you, and only you, to control access to Web content.

WARNING

If you forget your password, you'll never be able to go in and re-adjust the content settings in the future. *Write down your password* on a piece of paper and store it someplace where you'll be able to find it later!

6. Click the OK button.

Next, you'll be taken to the Content Advisor dialog box. If you click one of the rating scales, Language, Nudity, Sex, or Violence, a slider will appear beneath the list as in Figure 7.11. Initially, each scale is set to the strictest setting—only sites rated 0 on that scale are allowed to be viewed. As you drag the slider to the right, you allow more content through. In a sense, as you move the slider from left to right, you move from "rated G" to "rated X" content. You need to adjust the slider for each of the four scales.

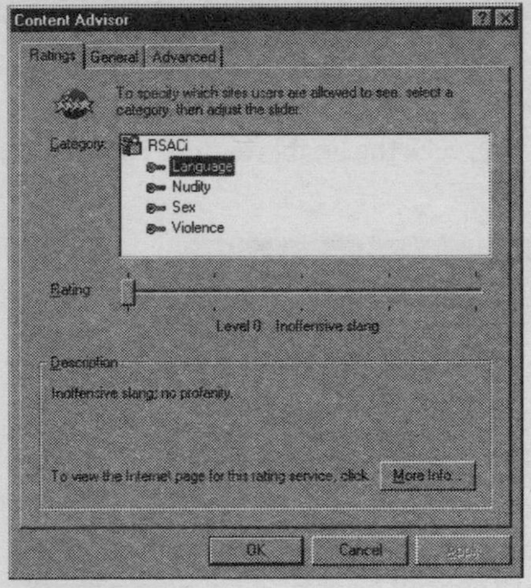

FIGURE 7.11: Choosing levels of acceptability in the Content Advisor dialog box

NOTE

To learn more about RASCi, click the More Info button or visit http://www.rsac.org.

To ensure that only sites that have been rated by RASCi are viewable, click the General tab and make sure the *Users can see sites that have no rating* checkbox is clear (unselected). Many sites, including the raunchiest, aren't rated at all. If you were to select that checkbox, your child could easily view those unsavory sites. The second option on that page allows the supervisor or parent to approve or disapprove of content on a page-by-page basis. When visiting a site that hasn't been rated, the dialog box below appears on the screen. The parent can type in the supervisor password and click OK to allow the page to be viewed or click the Cancel button or press Escape to prevent viewing.

After making your selections from the Content Advisor dialog box, close all open dialog boxes by clicking their OK buttons. You'll see a message stating that recently-viewed pages will still be accessible to kids. To get a clean start, close Internet Explorer by clicking its Close (x) button. Then re-start it in the usual manner. Your content settings will be enforced for every Web site you visit from then on.

Disabling Content Ratings

If you want to disable content ratings after the kids have gone to bed, follow these steps:

1. Choose View ➤ Internet Options from Internet Explorer's menu bar.

2. Click the Content tab.

3. Click the Disable button.

4. Enter your supervisor password and click the OK button.

A message appears, reminding you to turn the settings back on when you've finished your own browsing. Click the OK button to close the message box and then click the OK button to close the Internet Options dialog box. You can now browse the Web normally with no content restrictions.

To enable content settings again in the future, repeat steps 1-4 above, but choose Enable in Step 3. You can also choose Settings in step 3 if you want to change your content settings.

Blocking and Filtering Software

If Internet Explorer's content advisor doesn't quite cut it for you, there are other programs that you can use to block and filter Web content. Most offer some combination of the following features:

▶ Block access to inappropriate Web sites, chat rooms, and other sources.

▶ Rate sites based on adult content including pornography, profanity, violence, intolerance, militant extremists, gambling, drug culture, and so forth.

▶ Establish time controls for when kids can use the Internet.

▶ Keep track of where children have been on the Internet, including sites the child may have attempted to visit despite the program's blocking access to those sites.

All of these products have Web sites that you can visit to learn more. Most even let you download a free trial-version of the product so you can check it out yourself. Here's a list of products and Web sites you can visit to learn more:

Site Name	URL
Cyber Patrol	www.cyberpatrol.com
CyberSitter	www.cybersitter.com
CyberSnoop	www.pearlsw.com
Family Connect	www.familyconnect.com
Guardianet	www.guardiannet.net
Kids Protected Online	www.kpo.net
NetNanny	www.netnanny.com

Site Name	URL
Safe-Net Suite	www.maiasoftware.com/safenet
Surf Watch	www.surfwatch.com
SurfMonkey	www.surfmonkey.com
Web Sense	www.websense.com
WebChaperone	www.webchaperone.com
WinGuardian	www.webroot.com
WinWhatWhere For Families	www.winwhatwhere.com
WizGuard	www.wizguard.com
X-Stop	www.xstop.com

Filtering Services and ISPs

Another approach to shielding children from bad content is to sign up with an ISP that pre-filters content for you. Many of these services will add filtering to your existing account. Others can act as your one-and-only ISP. Table 7.1 lists the services, including the URL to visit, and phone numbers to call if you have no access to the Internet yet.

TABLE 7.1: Filtering Services and ISPs

SERVICE	URL	PHONE
Clean Internet	www.cleaninter.net	1(888)355-3113
ClearSail.Net	www.clearsail.net	1(888)905-0888
FamilyConnect	www.familyconnect.com	1(918)524-1010
Porn Blocker	www.pornblocker.com	1(888)564-7555
Rated-G Online	www.rated-g.com	1(704)544-7071
TrustedNet	www.trusted.net	1(800)347-2447

Parent and Teacher Support

If you're concerned about kids on the Internet, remember that you are certainly not alone. There are many resources on the Internet designed to help parents and teachers share their concerns and keep up with advances in technology. To explore some of those sites, stop by my home page at `http://www.coolnerds.com` and check out the links listed under Parent Resources or Educator Resources. You'll also find some fun sites listed under Family Fun.

Exploring the Explorer

I've probably told you more about the browsing the Web than you really need to know. Most people get by with just entering URLs, following hyperlinks, and occasionally adding a site to their list of favorites. Should you encounter any problems or want to explore other options, you might want to check out some of the following resources:

► To reinforce what you're learned in these last three chapters, try taking the online Web tutorial. Open Internet Explorer and choose Help ➢ Web Tutorial from its menu bar.

► For "local help" that you can access without being online, choose Help ➢ Contents And Index from Internet Explorer's menu bar. A standard Windows help dialog box will appear, providing information that's specifically relevant to Internet Explorer 4.

► To check and change settings for your Internet Explorer browser, choose View ➢ Internet Options from Internet Explorer's toolbar. You'll be taken to a dialog box where you can tweak settings to your liking.

► To see if there's any news or product updates for Internet Explorer, go to Microsoft's Internet Explorer Web page at `http://www.microsoft.com/ie40` or choose Help ➢ Product Updates from Internet Explorer's menu bar.

Good Things to Remember

The next chapter begins a whole new phase of this book where we'll look at using the Internet as a communications media, starting with the most popular of all services, e-mail. Before we move on, take a moment to review the main points covered in this chapter:

▶ To add a Web page to your collection of favorites, choose Favorites ➤ Add To Favorites from Internet Explorer's menu bar while viewing the page.

▶ To revisit a favorite site, choose Favorites from Internet Explorer's menu bar and then click site you want to revisit.

▶ To organize your collection of favorites into groups, choose Favorites ➤ Organize Favorites from Internet Explorer's menu bar.

▶ You can also access Favorites through the Explorer bar. Just click the Favorites button in Internet Explorer's toolbar or choose View ➤ Explorer Bar ➤ Favorites from Internet Explorer's menu bar.

▶ Subscriptions are a means of having your PC check for updates to pages while you're away from the computer.

▶ Internet Explorer's Content Advisor allows parents to limit kids to sites that have been rated by RASCi. There are also many third-party programs you can use to control kids' access to the Internet.

Chapter 8

DOING E-MAIL

A s you may already know, electronic mail (or *e-mail* for short) is a way of using the Internet as sort of a post office. You can type and send messages to anyone who has an e-mail address and you can receive messages from anyone who has access to the Internet. Unlike conventional mail, which costs money and usually takes a few days to get to its destination, e-mail is free and usually only takes a few seconds to reach its destination—no matter how far away the recipient may be. In this day and age where people never seem to answer telephones anymore, e-mail can be the perfect antidote for terminal telephone tag: Just fire off an e-mail message and wait for the response.

What You Need for E-Mail

To do e-mail, you need some kind of e-mail program. There are many available, including Microsoft Outlook Express, Microsoft Outlook, Netscape Mail, and Eudora. In this book we'll focus on Outlook Express because it comes with Windows, and therefore I can assume you already own it.

If you don't have Outlook Express on your PC, most likely it has never been installed. In that case, you can install it using the Windows Setup tab of Add/Remove Programs in the Windows Control Panel. You can also download a copy from `http://www.microsoft.com/msdownload` or `http://www.microsoft.com/ie40.htm`.

You will also need the following information from your Internet Service Provider (chances are you already jotted this information down back in Table 3.1 of Chapter 3—items 10 through 14 in that table):

▶ E-mail address used by people sending you mail

▶ Your incoming (POP, POP3, or IMAP) mail server

▶ Your outgoing (SMTP) mail server

▶ Your e-mail username

▶ Your e-mail password

> **FREE E-MAIL**
>
> In this chapter I'm assuming that you've signed up with an ISP that offers e-mail. If your Internet account doesn't provide e-mail, you can pick up a free account at http://www.hotmail.com or http://www.yahoo.com. However, the instructions presented in this chapter might not apply to those accounts. See the instructions at those Web sites for information on obtaining and using your free e-mail account.

Setting Up Outlook Express

Assuming you do plan to use Microsoft Outlook Express as your e-mail program, the first thing you need to do is set up your e-mail account. You should have already signed up with an ISP and set up your modem. Then, you can open Outlook Express, starting at the Windows desktop by using any of the following methods:

▶ Click the Windows Start button and choose Programs ➢ Internet Explorer ➢ Outlook Express.

▶ Open the Outlook Express icon, if available, on your Windows desktop.

▶ In Windows 98, click the Launch Outlook Express button in the Quick Launch toolbar.

The very first time you (or someone else) opens Outlook Express, a dialog box like the one below will appear, asking where you'd like to store your messages. You can just click the OK button to accept the suggested Outlook Express folder. If that dialog doesn't appear, don't worry about it. It just means that someone has already chosen a folder for storing messages.

When Outlook Express opens, it will look like Figure 8.1. Notice that like most Windows programs, Outlook Express appears within a window that you can move and size using the standard Windows techniques.

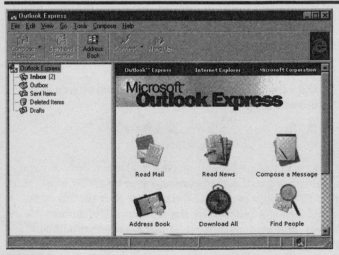

FIGURE 8.1:   Outlook Express, as it looks when first opened

Before you can use Outlook Express for e-mail, you need to set up an e-mail account, as described next.

Setting Up an E-Mail Account

Setting up an e-mail account in Outlook Express is pretty easy. And fortunately, you need only do it once. Here are the steps:

1. From the Outlook Express menu bar, choose Tools ➤ Accounts. A dialog box named Internet Accounts appears.

WARNING

It's possible that the Internet Connection Wizard has already set up your e-mail account. If so, you'll see the account name listed on the Mail tab of the Internet Accounts dialog box. If the account already exists, don't create it again! Just click the Close button to exit the dialog box and then skip down to the section titled "Sending Out E-Mail Messages."

2. Click the Add button in the Internet Accounts dialog box and choose Mail from the small submenu that appears.

3. The Internet Connection Wizard appears. The first page just asks for your name. Type in your name normally (for example, I would just type *Alan Simpson*) and then click the Next button.

4. The second Wizard page asks that you type in your e-mail address. This *must* be exactly the e-mail address provided by your ISP (item number 10 back in Table 3.1). Click the Next button after entering your e-mail address.

5. The third Wizard screen asks for information about your e-mail servers, as follows:

   ▶ Use the first option to choose whether your server is of the POP3 or IMAP variety. If you don't know, just choose POP3, as that is the most common, or ask your ISP which choice applies to your account.

   ▶ Type the name of your incoming mail server into the second option. This corresponds to item number 11 back in Table 3.1.

▶ Type the name of your outgoing mail server into the third option (item number 12 back in Table 3.1). The page should look something like the example below, but with your account information, rather than mine, filled in.

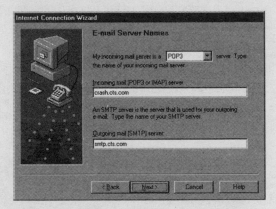

6. On the next Wizard page, fill in your e-mail (or POP) account name and password. These correspond to items 13 and 14 back in Table 3.1. Unless specifically instructed, leave the last item unselected as in the example below. Then click the Next button.

7. The next Wizard page asks for a "friendly name" for this account. You can accept the suggested name (which will be the name of your incoming mail server) or type in any name you like. Then click the Next > button to move on.

8. The next Wizard screen asks you to choose a connection type. Assuming you use a modem to connect to the Internet, choose the first option, *Connect using my phone line*, and then click the Next button.

9. The next Wizard screen will ask which dial-up networking connectoid you want to use to connect for e-mail. You can use the same one you use for the Web. For example, below I chose *Use an existing dial-up connection* and then I clicked on my CTS 56K account, which is the same one I use to browse the Web. Click Next after making your selection.

10. Finally, you come to the last Wizard page, which is just a congratulatory message. Click the Finish button to return to the Internet Accounts dialog box. If you click the Mail tab in that dialog box, you should see your new e-mail account listed there. Click the Close button near the bottom of that dialog box to return to Outlook Express.

Hooray, you're done! Now you can send and receive e-mail just like anyone else on the Internet. Outlook Express offers lots of options for sending and receiving e-mail. But before we get too detailed, let's cover the two most important topics first—how to send an e-mail message and how to read e-mail messages that others have sent to you.

Sending E-Mail Messages

Composing (writing) an e-mail message and sending it to someone is a simple procedure. Here are the steps:

1. Choose Compose ➢ New Message from the Outlook Express menu bar or just click the Compose Message button in the toolbar.

NOTE

The Compose Message button in the toolbar is disabled (dimmed) unless you click the Inbox, Outbox, or some other folder name in the left column of the Outlook Express Window.

2. In the New Message dialog box that appears, type the recipient's e-mail address next to To:. For example, in Figure 8.2, I've addressed the e-mail to my own `alan@cts.com` account.

3. Click the Subject option and type in a brief description of the message you're sending. This description will appear in the recipient's e-mail program. In the sample shown in Figure 8.2, I've typed the description "Just Testing."

4. Click the large white area and then type your e-mail message. You may also want to type your return e-mail address, as I've done in Figure 8.2.

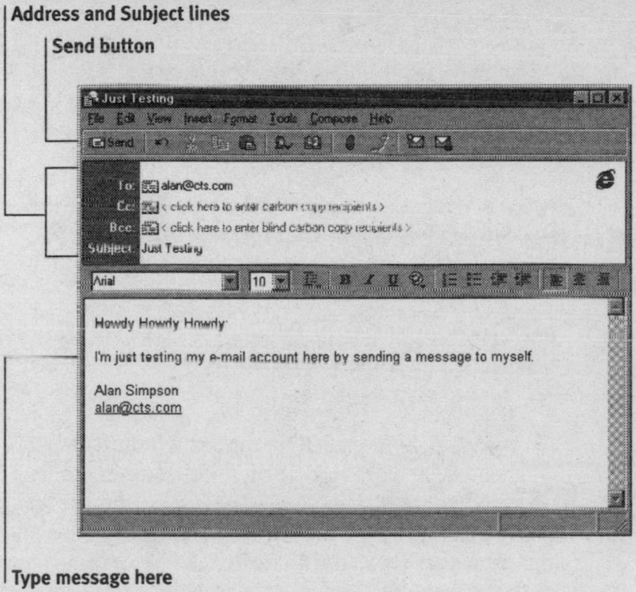

Address and Subject lines

Send button

Type message here

FIGURE 8.2:   A sample e-mail message I'm composing

5. When you've finished composing your message, click the Send button near the upper left corner of the New Message dialog box.

You will be returned to Outlook Express. Most likely, your computer will connect to the Internet and send the message immediately. You'll have to wait for it to make the connection and send the message. But if your message isn't sent right away, don't worry about it. As I'll explain under "Noteworthy Options" later in this chapter, you can opt to have Outlook Express hold onto your outgoing messages and then send them all in one fell swoop, which in turn keeps you from having to wait for each message to be sent individually.

E-MAIL ETIQUETTE

Netiquette (network etiquette) is sort of an unofficial set of rules that define what is, and isn't, cool to do on the Internet. There are a few rules of netiquette that apply to e-mail, as summarized below:

▶ When creating an e-mail message, don't leave the Subject line blank. Outlook Express will allow you to do it, but recipients often find the practice irritating.

▶ Never use all uppercase letters to type a message. IT LOOKS LIKE YOU'RE SHOUTING.

▶ If you can't spell worth beans, spell-check your message before clicking the Send button. If you have Microsoft Word on your PC, you can use its spell-checker. Just choose Tools ≻ Spelling from the Outlook Express menu bar. Otherwise, use a dictionary (yeah, fat chance, right?).

▶ Never, ever send out *spam* (junk mail that the recipient didn't request). You'll surely get *flamed* (get a whole lot of nasty messages in reply).

Unfortunately, not everyone goes along with the last item. So you're likely to get junk mail in your own e-mail inbox from time to time. If you really hate junk mail and would like to join the crusade to end spamming, check out some of the anti-spamming sites on the World Wide Web. Use Internet Explorer and your favorite search engine to locate pages dealing with *spam* or *anti-spam*.

Sending to Multiple Recipients

You're not limited to sending your message to a single recipient. You can use the cc: (carbon copy) box to list e-mail addresses of persons you'd like to send a copy of the message to. If you don't want the person who is getting the copy to see all the other recipients' addresses, use the bcc (blind carbon copy) box instead. If you want to put multiple e-mail addresses on any one line, just separate the addresses with a comma (,) or semicolon (;).

Reading Your E-Mail Messages

Any e-mail messages that are sent to you initially are stored on your ISP's e-mail server. To read your messages, you first need to get them off that server and onto your own PC. Initially, all new messages will appear in your inbox folder in Outlook Express. Here's how to get your message off the server and into your inbox:

1. If you've closed Outlook Express, re-open it.

2. Click the Send And Receive button on the Outlook Express toolbar or choose Tools ➢ Download All from the Outlook Express menu bar.

3. A large dialog box will appear, keeping you informed of the download progress. When that dialog box disappears, any new messages you've received will be stored in your Inbox.

To view your messages, click the Inbox folder in the left column of the Outlook Express window, as in Figure 8.3. The column on the right then splits into two panes. The top pane is the *message list*, which lists the sender and subject of every message in your inbox. Message lines shown in boldface are messages you've never read. The rest are messages that you've already read, but left in your inbox.

NOTE

The first two messages shown in Figure 8.3, shown as being from Microsoft Outlook, are just samples provided by Microsoft. Any "real" messages will be listed under those two.

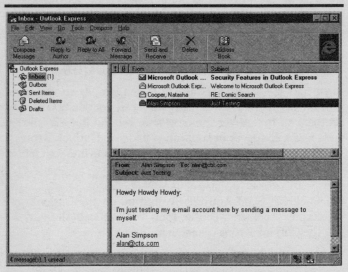

FIGURE 8.3: Viewing my Inbox folder in Outlook Express

To read a specific message, click it in the top pane. The bottom pane shows the actual content of that message. For example, in Figure 8.3, I've already clicked *Inbox* in the left pane. The number *1* enclosed in parentheses to the right of the Inbox folder name indicates that there is one unread message in that folder. In the message list (top pane), I've clicked on the bottom message—the one from Alan Simpson with the subject *Just Testing*. (That's the sample message I e-mailed to myself). The body of that message appears in the lower pane.

EMOTICONS AND ACRONYMS

Internet users have developed some abbreviations to help keep typing to a minimum. Some of the more common ones, which may well appear in messages you receive, are listed below:

:-) Smiley—an emoticon (emotion icon) that means "just kidding" or "a joke." If you turn the page sideways it looks like two eyes, a nose, and a smiling mouth.

<g> or **<gr>** Stands for "grin." Like the smiley, it means "just kidding" or "no offense."

BTW By the way.

IMHO In my humble opinion.

LOL Laughing out loud.

ROTFL Rolling on the floor laughing.

RTFM Read the f***ing manual.

TIA Thanks in advance.

TLA Three-letter aconym.

After you've read a message, you need to decide what you want to do with it. In a nutshell, your choices are:

▶ Respond to the person who sent you the message.

▶ Print the message.

▶ File the message away for future reference.

▶ Forward the message to someone else.

▶ Trash the message.

The next sections describe how to do those things.

Replying to a Message

After you read an e-mail message, you may want to respond to the person who sent you that message. In that case, there's no need to compose an entirely new message from scratch. Instead, you can just click the Reply To Author button on the Outlook Express toolbar. A window appears with the recipient's name already typed into the To: line. (The recipient's actual e-mail address may not appear, but it's in there.)

All you need to do is type your reply into the large white area, above the *Original Message* stuff. And don't worry about that original message—it's just there as a reminder to the person you're replying to, in case they need to review the message they sent you in order to understand the context of your reply. When you've finished typing your reply message, click the Send button near the upper left corner of the message window.

Printing a Message

To print the message that you're currently reading, choose File ➤ Print from the Outlook Express menu bar. Then click the OK button in the Print dialog box that appears.

Filing for Future Reference

If you want to get a message out of your inbox, but don't want to trash it, you can set it aside in some other folder. Here's how:

1. Using the message list (top pane) of Outlook Express, right-click the message you want to file away.

2. Choose Move To from the menu that appears. The Move dialog box appears.

3. If you want to create a new folder for storing messages like the current one, click the New Folder button, type in a folder name, and then click the OK button.

4. Click the name of the folder you want to put the message into and then click the OK button.

You might find it useful to set up several folders for storing messages, as in the example shown in the left pane of Figure 8.4. Doing so will make it easier to browse through all the messages you've received regarding any given topic.

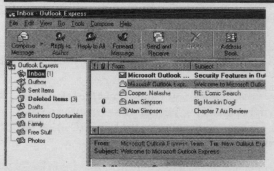

FIGURE 8.4: Sample folders in the left pane of Outlook Express, used for filing e-mail messages by topic

TIP
You can also create a folder on-the-fly in the left pane of Outlook Express. Just right-click the icon labeled Outlook Express at the top of the folder list and choose New Folder. Type in a folder name and click the OK button.

Forwarding a Message

If you want to pass an e-mail message you've received on to someone else, you can forward the message. While viewing the message, click the Forward Message button on the Outlook Express toolbar or choose Compose ➢ Forward. Type the recipient's e-mail address in the To: box of the window that appears and then click the Send button near the upper left corner of that same dialog box.

Deleting a Message

When you've finished reading a message in your inbox, you can
delete it. Doing so will keep your inbox from becoming filled with
thousands of old messages. There are a couple ways to delete a
message. Just use whichever method is most convenient for you
at the moment:

▶ In the top right pane of Outlook Express, right-click the
   message you want to delete and choose Delete from the
   menu that appears.

▶ Make sure the message you want to delete is selected in
   that top right pane. Then click the Delete button on the
   Outlook Express toolbar or press the Delete (Del) key on
   your keyboard.

By default, deleted messages are just moved into the folder
named Deleted Items. That gets them out of your inbox, which
helps keep that box from becoming cluttered with old messages.
Those messages, however, remain on your hard disk and continue
to eat up disk space. To view deleted messages at any time, click
the Deleted Items folder in the left column of Outlook Express.
The right panes now show only deleted messages. You can do any
of the following with those deleted messages:

▶ To read a deleted message, click it. The contents of that
   message appear in the lower pane.

▶ To "undelete" a message, right-click the message line in
   the top pane, choose Move To from the menu that appears,
   choose Inbox (or any other folder name), and click the OK
   button.

▶ To permanently delete a message so that it no longer
   resides on your hard disk, right-click the message line
   in the top pane and choose Delete. You'll see a message
   asking if you're sure you want to permanently delete the
   message. Choose Yes.

WARNING

Once you delete a message from the Deleted Items folder, there's no way to get it back. So be careful!

If you want to clean out your Deleted Items folder altogether, thereby permanently deleting all the old messages in there, click the Deleted Items folder in the left pane of Outlook Express. Then, click the first message listed in the top right pane to select it. Next, scroll down to the bottom message in the right pane, hold down the Shift key, and click the last message. All the messages in the Deleted Items folder will now be selected. To permanently delete the whole kit and caboodle, just click the Delete button in the toolbar or press the Delete (Del) key on your keyboard.

Attaching Files to Messages

One of the best features of e-mail is the fact that you're not limited to sending typed messages to other people: You can send virtually any file on your PC—be it a digital photo, a document you typed, a spreadsheet, or whatever—to the recipient as well. In fact, you can tack a whole bunch of files to a message if you like. The procedure is easy:

1. In Outlook Express, address and compose your e-mail message in the usual manner.

2. To attach a file to the message, click the Insert File (paper clip) button on the Outlook Express toolbar or choose Insert ➢ File Attachment from the Outlook Express menu bar. The Insert Attachment dialog box shown in Figure 8.5 appears.

3. Use the Look In drop-down list at the top of the dialog box or the files and folder list in the larger pane to open the folder that contains the file you want to send.

4. When you find the file you want to attach, click its name and then click the Attach button in the Insert Attachment dialog box.

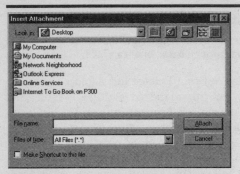

FIGURE 8.5: The Insert Attachment dialog box

The attachment appears as an icon, with a filename and size, below the body of the message, as shown in Figure 8.6. Then click the Send button near the upper right corner of the message window, as usual, and you're done.

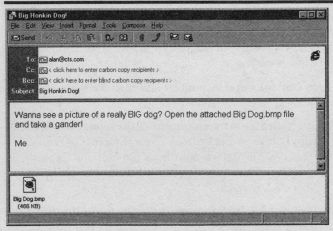

FIGURE 8.6: This e-mail message has a file named Big Dog.bmp attached to it.

Opening Received Attachments

Other people can send attachments to you. When viewing messages in your inbox, the ones with attachments will have a little paper clip icon to the left of the sender's name. When viewing the body of such a message (as shown in Figure 8.7), the top part of the message also sports a large paper clip. Clicking that larger paper clip, as I've done in the figure, displays the name and size of the attached file (or files, there may be several).

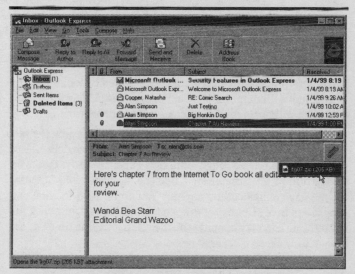

FIGURE 8.7: Message in my inbox with a file attached to it

To open or save the attached file, you must first click that large paper clip. Then click the name of the file you want to open or save. The dialog box shown below appears.

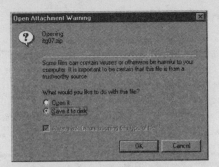

To view the attached file immediately, without putting a copy on your hard disk, choose Open It. Windows will attempt to open the file, using whichever program on your PC is best suited for the job. It determines which program is best suited by looking at the attachment's filename extension. For example, a file with a .doc extension will be opened in Microsoft Word or WordPad.

If no program on your computer is suitable for opening the file, then you'll see a message like the one below. Not much help, unless you happen to have enough Windows expertise to "...create an association in My Computer..." like the message says. Actually, the message is misleading anyway. You don't need to create an association in My Computer to open the file. Instead, just click the OK button. Then try opening the file again, but this time choose Save it To Disk, as discussed next.

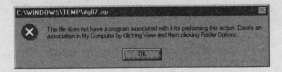

To save the attached file as a file on your hard disk, choose Save It To Disk. When the Save Attachment As dialog box appears, be sure to select a folder from the Save In drop-down list to indicate where you want to put the file. I suggest that you use either the Desktop folder, as in the example below, or My Documents. If you choose the Desktop folder, the file's icon will be plainly visible on your Windows desktop, where you're not likely to lose track of it. If you choose My Documents, you can easily get to the file's icon by opening the My Documents folder from the Windows desktop.

Once the attached file is saved to disk, you can open it by clicking (or double-clicking) its icon on the Windows desktop or via Windows' My Computer, Windows Explorer, or Find command. The file will open in whichever program is best suited for that type of file.

If the file won't open and you end up in the Open With dialog box (shown below), then Windows doesn't know which program would be best suited to viewing the file's contents. You need to decide for yourself which of the programs listed in the box would be best suited for the file. If you don't have a clue as to what that might be, let me make some suggestions:

▶ If you think the attached file contains a picture, choose a graphics program such as KodakImg, MSPaint, or any other graphics program in the list. Then click the OK button.

▶ If you think the attached file contains text, choose Word-Pad or some word processing program from the list. This selection usually works with files that have the .att (attachment) filename extension. Then click the OK button.

▶ If the file has a .zip extension, you cannot open it until you get a zip program such as WinZip, discussed in the "Zip Files" sidebar below.

Notice the checkbox labeled *Always use this program to open this file*. If you leave that checkbox filled, you'll automatically set up an association between that filename extension and the program you chose to open that file with. There's no need to "...create an association in My Computer..." Any time you click (or double-click) a filename with the same filename extension as the current file, Windows will automatically open that file with whichever program you selected from the list.

ZIP FILES

It's a fairly common practice among e-mailers to compress, or *zip*, files before sending them as attachments. Doing so reduces the size of the file, which in turn allows for faster transfers. Zipping files can also help reduce the likelihood of the file being corrupted (damaged) during the transfer.

To zip files you plan to send, as well as to unzip compressed files that have been sent to you, you'll need some kind of zip program. I use a product named WinZip. You can download a free shareware evaluation copy of that program yourself from www.winzip.com. Use your Internet Explorer program to go that URL, then follow the instructions on that site to locate and download WinZip.

Attached Pictures

If someone attaches one or more photos or other pictures to a message they send you, those pictures might already be opened at the bottom of the message so you can view the photo immediately without opening any icons. If you receive such an attachment, you can still save a copy of that item to your hard disk. Just right-click the picture and choose Save File As from the menu that appears. In the Save Picture dialog box that appears, choose a folder to put the photo in (e.g., My Documents). Note the filename (or change it of you like) so you can easily find the file later. Then click the Save button. A copy of the photo is saved to your hard disk, and the original copy remains in the e-mail message.

Your E-Mail Address Book

Outlook Express has its own address book, which you can use to keep track of people's e-mail addresses. You can automate things so that some names are added to the address book automatically, as I'll discuss next.

Adding Names to the Address Book

The best way to use the address book is to first set it up so that each time you reply to some message, that person's e-mail address is automatically added to the address book. Here's how to set that option:

1. From the Outlook Express menu bar, choose Tools ➤ Options.

2. On the General tab, select (check) the Automatically Put People I Reply To In My Address Book option.

3. Click the OK button near the bottom of the dialog box.

That's one way to start filling your address book. Another way is to open the address book and type in names and e-mail addresses manually. Here's how:

1. Click the Address Book button on the Outlook Express toolbar or choose Tools ➤ Address Book from the Outlook Express menu bar. The Address Book opens, as shown in Figure 8.8. (In that example I haven't added any names and addresses to the address book yet.)

2. To add a person to the address book, click the New Contact button in the address book's toolbar.

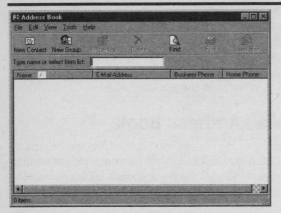

FIGURE 8.8: The Windows Address Book

3. In the dialog box that appears, fill in the person's name
and e-mail address in the boxes provided. For example,
in Figure 8.9, I set up an e-mail address for a person
named Ashley Simpson at `ashley@coolnerds.com`.

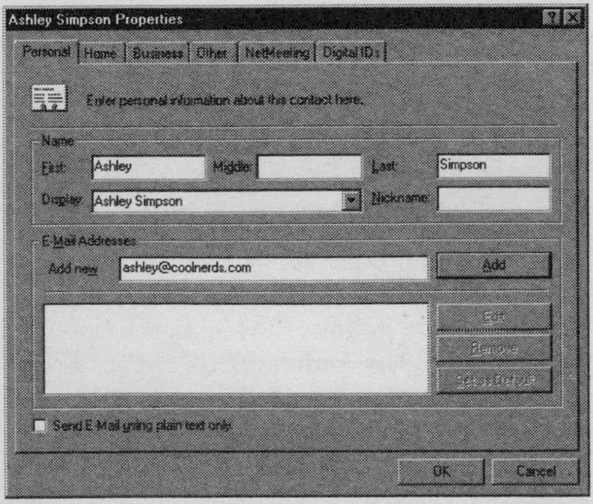

FIGURE 8.9: New contact added to the address book

4. Alternatively, you can click the Home, Business, or other tabs to enter additional information about this person. However, if you already have some other means of storing that information, you might want to use this address book to keep track of e-mail addresses only.

5. Click the OK button to return to the address book.

6. Repeat steps 2-5 to add as many names and e-mail addresses as you like.

When you've finished adding a name (or names) to the address book, go ahead and close it in the usual manner. That is, click the Close (X) button in the upper right corner of the address book window or choose File ➢ Close from the Address Book's menu bar.

Using the Address Book

Once you have some names and addresses in your address book, you can use it to address your e-mail messages. Here's how:

1. In Outlook Express, click the Compose Message to start typing a new message.

2. Rather than typing the recipient's e-mail address into the To: portion of the message, click the rolodex card icon to the right of the word *To:*. The Select Recipients address book opens.

3. In the list of names that appears, click the intended recipient's name and then click the To:-> button. Note that you can select as many recipients as you wish in this manner. You can also add names to the cc: and bcc: lines via the address book.

4. Click the OK button.

Don't be alarmed if the recipient's name, rather than e-mail address, appears in the To: portion of your message. Outlook Express will automatically use that person's e-mail address, rather than the name, to send the message.

If at any time you need to get into your address book and change information about a person, or delete them, go back into Outlook Express and choose Tools ➤ Address Book from its menu bar once again to reopen the address book. To change a person's information, click their name and then click the Properties button in the toolbar. To delete a person, click their name and then click the Delete button in the address book's toolbar.

Making Your Own Stationery

It's always a good idea to type your name and e-mail address at the bottom of every message you send. Better yet, you can create your own e-mail stationery that already has that information in it. Here's how:

1. From the Outlook Express menu bar, choose Tools ➤ Stationery.

2. Click the Signature button in the dialog box that appears.

3. In the Signature dialog box, which appears next, choose the first option, *Add this signature to all outgoing messages*.

4. Select the Text option and type in your signature lines. For example, Figure 8.10 shows a signature line sporting my name, my preferred e-mail address, and my Web site's URL.

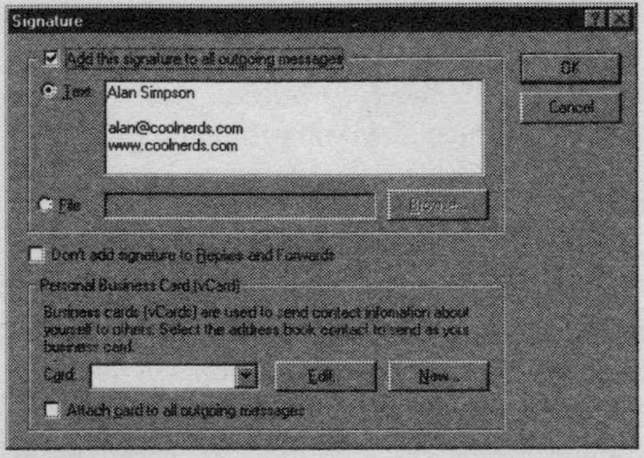

FIGURE 8.10: Signature lines to be added to all my messages

5. After typing your signature line(s), click the OK button to close the current dialog box, then click the OK button to close the next dialog box.

The next time you compose a new e-mail message, you'll see your signature line already typed in at the bottom of the message.

Noteworthy Options

There are still more options to choose from in Outlook Express. To get to these options, choose Tools > Options from the Outlook Express menu bar. The Options dialog box opens with the General tab selected, as shown in Figure 8.11. Here are some quick tips on choosing options that might make your e-mailing easier:

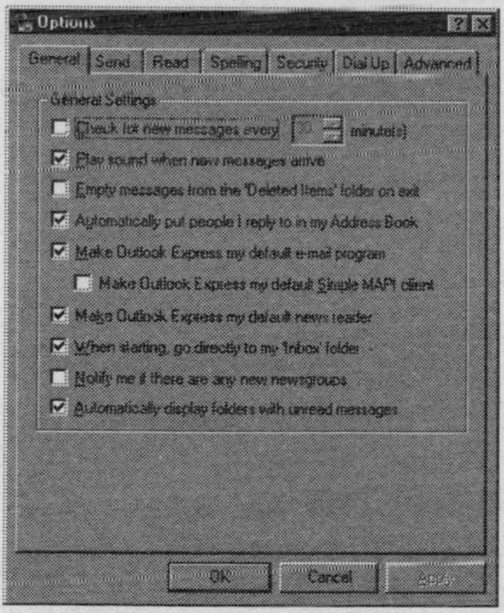

FIGURE 8.11: The Outlook Express Options dialog box

▶ To prevent Outlook Express from automatically dialing and checking for messages, clear the first option's checkbox, *Check for new messages every x minutes*. Then use the Send And Receive button to get and send mail at your own convenience. To have Outlook Express go straight to your Inbox when you first open it, select the *When start-ing, go directly to my "Inbox" folder* option. Very handy!

▶ To keep a copy of every message you send out, select the *Save copy of sent messages in the Sent Items folder*. That way, if you ever want to review some message that you sent in the past, you can just open the Sent Items folder in the left pane of Outlook Express.

▶ The *Send messages immediately* option determines when messages you send are actually sent out to the Internet. If you deselect (clear) this option, then all messages will be sent together when you click the Send And Receive button or choose Tools ➢ Send And Receive ➢ Send All from the menu.

▶ The *Automatically complete e-mail addresses when com-posing* enables the "auto-complete" feature, similar to the one described for Internet Explorer. As you type an e-mail address into the To: box of a message, Outlook Express will automatically complete the address based on known addresses in your address book.

Like most programs, Outlook Express has it's own help system. To get help in Outlook Express, just press the F1 key or choose Help ➢ Contents And Index from the Outlook Express menu bar. It even has its own Troublshooters built into that help system.

Good Things to Remember

That pretty much covers all the features of Outlook Express that have to do with e-mail. We'll be visiting Outlook Express again in Chapter 9, where you'll learn to use Outlook Express to partici-pate in yet another service of the Internet known as Usenet News-groups. Before we move on, let's take a moment to review the most important points covered in this chapter:

▶ Microsoft Outlook Express, which comes with Windows, is the program to use when you want to send or receive Internet e-mail.

▶ To compose a new e-mail message in Outlook Express, click the Compose Message in its toolbar or choose Compose ➤ New Message from its menu bar.

▶ When you've finished addressing and typing your e-mail message, click the Send button near the upper right corner of the New Message dialog box.

▶ E-mail messages you receive are stored in your Inbox folder. Click that folder's name to view your messages.

▶ To manually send and receive messages in Outlook Express, just click the Send And Receive button on the Outlook Express toolbar.

▶ To control exactly how and when Outlook Express connects to the Internet, adjust settings in its Options dialog box, which you can open by choosing Tools ➤ Options from the Outlook Express toolbar.

Chapter 9

You've Got a Friend in Newsgroups and Mailing Lists

Usenet newsgroups are yet another feature of the Internet. This particular feature gets the "most inappropriately named" award because despite the name, newsgroups have little or nothing to do with news. A more appropriate name would have been "discussion groups," because that's what people do in newsgroups. They discuss topics of mutual interest, newsworthy or not. Similar to newsgroups are *mailing lists*, which also provide a means of engaging in heated debates over whatever gets your goat. This chapter, as you may have guessed, is all about participating in newsgroups and mailing lists.

Why Mess with Newsgroups?

As mentioned, newsgroups are really more like discussion groups. Doing newsgroups is sort of like doing e-mail. In fact, you can use Outlook Express as your *news reader* (a program that lets you participate in newsgroups). However, unlike e-mail, where your message gets sent to one person, the message you send to a newsgroup might be seen by thousands of people. Any one of those people can reply to your message, just as an individual can reply to the e-mail message you send them.

Probably the best use of newsgroups is getting free answers to burning questions. For example, let's say you're thinking about buying a new car. You have a particular make and model Toyota in mind. Before making your final decision, you'd like to know whether existing owners of that car are satisfied.

First, you would want to find one or more newsgroups where people discuss Toyotas. Then, you could just send an e-mail message to that newsgroup saying you're thinking of buying this car and would like to know if current owners are happy with their purchase.

All the members of that newsgroup will see your message and some will certainly respond. Within a day or two, probably, you'll have a whole lot of honest answers from genuine owners, to further help you make your decision.

Newsgroup Jargon

Like all other things computer-ish, newsgroupies have their own language for describing things. Here's a quick rundown of the more common buzzwords:

▶ Each message in a newsgroup is officially called an *article* or a *post*, though just about everyone refers to them as *messages* because in a sense, they are like normal e-mail messages.

▶ A series of articles on the same subject is called a *thread*.

▶ Many newsgroups are *moderated* by people who weed out articles that are irrelevant to the group or that are just plain obnoxious. Most newsgroups, however, are *unmoderated*, which means anything goes.

▶ *Lurking* is hanging around a newsgroup to see what's being discussed. But unlike lurking around public parks at night, which is generally not good, lurking in a newsgroup is OK, particularly if you're new to the group.

▶ *Spamming* is posting articles that are really advertisements. Don't do it, or you're likely to get *flamed*.

▶ *Flaming* is sending nasty messages to people in the group.

▶ A *poster*, in newsgroup argot, isn't something you hang on a wall. It's a person who posts articles to the group.

Newsgroup Categories

There are tens of thousands of newsgroups on the Internet. The groups are divided into categories and subcategories. A single newsgroup's name generally follow the pattern:

```
category.subcategory.sub-subcategory
```

For example, the newsgroup `alt.animals.dogs` is a newsgroup where people who are interested in dogs can gather. There are thousands of categories out there. Some of the more widely used categories are listed in Table 9.1.

TABLE 9.1: Some Newsgroup Main Categories, Descriptions,
and Names

MAIN CATEGORY	DESCRIPTION	SAMPLE NEWSGROUP NAMES
Alt	Alternative lifestyles and topics.	alt.astrology.metapsych alt.beer
Bionet	Biology	bionet.genome bionet.jobs.offered
Biz	Business	biz.marketplace biz.entreprenuers
Comp	Computers	comp.graphics comp.internet
Law	Legal matters	law.court.federal law.school.crim
Misc	Miscellaneous	misc.activism misc.computers.forsale
News	Usenet news network	news.newusers news.newusers.questions
Rec	Recreation	rec.sport.football rec.photo.digital
Sci	Science	sci.bio.botany sci.med.midwifery
Soc	Social issues	soc.culture.hawaii soc.geneology
Talk	Debates and opinions	talk.bizarre talk.politics

Setting Up your News Reader

Outlook Express, that same program you use for e-mail, can also
act as your news reader. Provided that your ISP offers a news server,
or NNTP server as it's also called (where NNTP stands for Network News Transfer Protocol). If your ISP does have a news server,
you should have written that server's name down as item number
16 back in Table 3.1 of Chapter 3. If your ISP doesn't offer a news

server, then you can skip all the way down to the section titled "Accessing Newsgroups via the Web" to learn how to use your Web browser (Microsoft Internet Explorer) to access newsgroups.

Assuming your ISP has given you the address of a local news server, here's how you go about setting up Outlook Express to access that server:

1. Open Outlook Express as you normally would.

2. Choose Tools ➤ Accounts from the Outlook Express menu bar. The Internet Accounts dialog box appears.

WARNING

The Internet Connection Wizard may have already set up a news account for you. To find out, click the News tab in the Internet Accounts dialog box. If you see an account listed, just click the Close button and skip to the section titled "Downloading Newsgroups."

3. Click the Add button in the Internet Accounts dialog box and then choose News from the menu that appears. The Internet Connection Wizard appears.

4. On the first Wizard page, type your name normally (it may already be there, from when you set up your e-mail account) and then click the Next button.

5. On the second Wizard page, type your e-mail address. Again, it may already be there from earlier. Click the Next button.

6. On the next Wizard page, type in the name of your news server as provided by your ISP (item number 16 from Table 3.1). In Figure 9.1, I've typed in my ISP's news server name.

7. If your ISP requires that you log onto the server, and you have an NNTP account name and password, select (check) the *My news server requires me to log on* option. Then click the Next button and fill in your news account name and password.

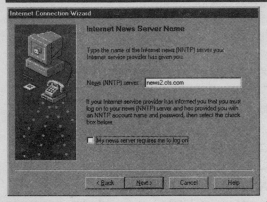

FIGURE 9.1: The Internet News Server Name page of the Internet Connection Wizard

8. Click the Next button and then fill in a "friendly" name for this new server (you could also just keep the suggested name). Then click the Next button.

9. In the next Wizard screen, choose *Connect using my phone line* (assuming you use a modem to access the Internet). Then click the Next button.

10. In the next Wizard screen, choose *Use an existing dial-up connection* and then click the dial-up connectoid you normally use to connect to the Internet. Click the Next button.

11. You should now be at the final congratulatory screen. Click the Finish button.

12. You're returned to the Internet Accounts dialog box. Click its Close button.

You will probably see a message asking if you'd like to download newsgroups from the news server you just added. If so, go ahead and click the Yes button. If prompted to connect to your server, go ahead and do so. Then wait a few minutes for all the newsgroups to be downloaded to your PC. When the download is finished, you'll see a long list of newsgroups named in the Newsgroups dialog box. For now, you can just close the Newsgroups dialog box by clicking the OK button near the bottom of that dialog box.

NOTE

Though it's called "downloading newsgroups," all you're really doing at this time is downloading the names of newsgroups that are available on your ISP's news server. So don't worry about your hard disk being filled up with all the messages from all those newsgroups.

If, for whatever reason, you can't download newsgroups right now, don't worry about it. You can download them at any time, as discussed under "Downloading Newsgroups" later in this chapter.

When you return to Outlook Express, you'll see a new folder in your folders list with the "friendly name" you gave to your news server. For example, in Figure 9.2 my news server name, news2 .cts.com, appears at the bottom of the folder list.

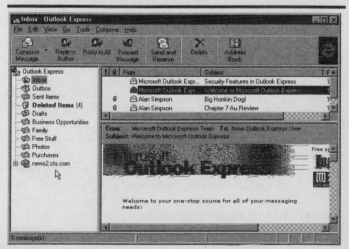

FIGURE 9.2: News server added to my folder list

Once the newsgroup name appears in your folder list, you want to remember this important point: *Whenever you want to do anything involving newsgroups, you'll want to click that folder first* or choose Go ≻ News from the Outlook Express menu bar. The Outlook Express toolbar changes when you do, offering a new button titled News Groups. As you'll see in the sections that follow, that one little button gives you access to all the newsgroups on your ISP's news server.

Downloading Newsgroups

In most situations, Outlook Express will automatically download newsgroup names from your news server as soon as you establish the connection to that server. But if, for whatever reason, you were unable to download newsgroups or if you want to re-load newsgroups to see if there are any new ones, follow these steps to update your list of newsgroups manually:

1. In the Outlook Express folder list, click the name of your news server and then click the News Groups button on the Outlook Express title bar. The Newsgroups dialog box appears.

2. To update your list of newsgroups, click the Reset List button.

It might take several minutes to download all the newsgroup names, so be patient. When the download is complete, you should see the names of newsgroup listed in the large white area of the Newsgroups dialog box. For example, Figure 9.3 shows how my Newsgroups dialog box looks after downloading newsgroups from my ISP. There are over 40,000 newsgroups in the list—only the top few are visible, though. Use the scrollbar to the right of the newsgroup names, your mouse wheel, or the Page Up and Page Down keys to scroll through the entire list.

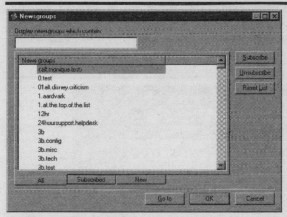

FIGURE 9.3: My Newsgroups dialog box after downloading news-groups from my ISP's news server

Finding Newsgroups that Interest You

Nobody has time to check out all the messages in 40,000 or so newsgroups. So the first thing you'll probably want to do is narrow the list down to a few newsgroups that discuss topics that are of interest to you. That's easy to do:

1. If you've left Outlook's Newsgroups dialog box, get back to it by clicking the News Groups button on the Outlook Express toolbar.

WARNING

Don't forget that the News Groups button on the Outlook Express toolbar is available *only* when the name of your news server is selected in the folders list.

2. In the *Display newsgroups which contain* box, type the word that best describes your interests. For example, if you play the banjo, you might type the word *banjo*.

The list of newsgroups in the dialog box shrinks to show only newsgroups that contain the topic you typed. For example, in Figure 9.4, I typed the word *banjo*, and now only newsgroup names that contain that word appear in the list.

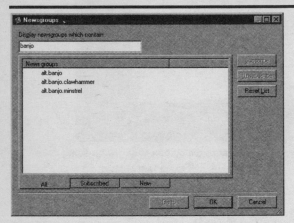

FIGURE 9.4:   The Newsgroups dialog box showing names of newsgroups that contain the word *banjo*

Beginner's Newsgroups

As a beginner, you might want to check out some of the groups that are designed for newbies. If you type the phrase *news.newusers* into the *Display newsgroups which contain* box, you'll see the groups that are geared toward newbies, perhaps looking like the example in Figure 9.5. (Your news server might offer different groups.)

Previewing Newsgroup Messages

Before you decide whether you want to get involved in a newsgroup, you should lurk around and check out some of the articles within the newsgroup. Here's how to do that:

1. If you're not already in the Newsgroups dialog box, click the News Groups button on the Outlook Express toolbar to get back there.

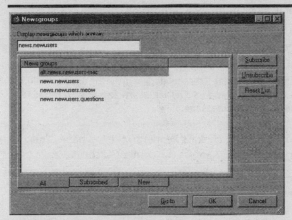

FIGURE 9.5: Groups geared toward newsgroup newbies

2. Click the All tab near the bottom of the Newsgroups dialog box to make sure you're viewing the complete list of newsgroups.

3. If you haven't already done so, type some word in the *Display newsgroups which contain* text box to narrow the list of newsgroup names to those that discuss a topic that interest you.

4. To see the messages in a newsgroup, click its name and then click the Go To button near the bottom of the Newsgroups dialog box.

NOTE

If the Go To button doesn't bring you any messages, you're probably working offline. Click the Connect button on the Outlook Express toolbar and connect to the Internet normally. Messages headers should appear in the top pane after the connection is made.

5. The Newsgroup dialog box disappears and you're returned to Outlook Express. The message list pane now contains

a list of articles in the newsgroup you selected. As with
e-mail, unread articles are shown in boldface.

NOTE

In newsgroups, the lines that appear in the top pane are referred
to as message *headers*. The actual article is often referred to as
the *body* of the message.

6. To read a message, click its header in the top pane. The
bottom preview pane shows the content of the message.

7. If there are any responses to the message you're viewing,
the message line in the top pane will have a + sign next
to it. Click that + sign to expand the line and view a list
of replies. Click any reply to view its message.

In Figure 9.6, I opted to view the news.newusers.questions
newsgroup. Notice the message lines at the top of the dialog box.
If you look closely, you'll see that the message I'm viewing at the
moment poses a question about downloading Web pages. The
indented messages beneath that message are replies—answers sent
to the group in direct response to the groupie's question. You can
always tell which questions already have been answered by the +
sign just to left of that message line. Clicking the + sign displays
the message lines for those replies.

TIP

You can adjust the width of any column in the list of message
headers by dragging, left or right, the dark line that separates
the column headings. For example, to widen or narrow the Subject column, drag the dark line that's just to the right of the
Subject column heading.

To read any message in the list of headers, just click the header
of the message you want to read. Outlook Express will (probably) download the body of that message from the news server and

display it in the lower preview pane. I say "probably" because it depends on certain settings, which may have been adjusted by someone else on your PC.

Instead of a message, you might see an instruction to "Press **<Space>** to display the selected message." You need to press the space bar on your keyboard to download that message. If pressing the space bar still doesn't bring the body of the message into the preview pane, you're probably no longer connected to your news server. Click the Connect button in Outlook Express to re-connect to your ISP's news server.

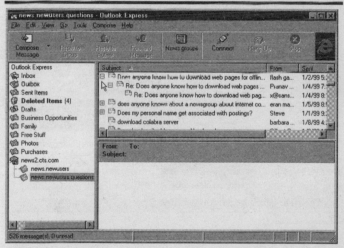

FIGURE 9.6:   Viewing a newsgroup's message headers in Outlook Express

Spend a few minutes looking through the messages and replies in any newsgroup that you think might interest you. If you like what you see and you think that you might like to visit this news-group often, you can *subscribe* to the group to make future access even easier.

Subscribing to Newsgroups

Subscribing to a newsgroup is simple and free. There are two ways to subscribe to a group. Use whichever is most convenient at the moment:

▶ If you've already previewed the group, and its name appears under your news server name in the folders list, right-click the newsgroup name and choose Subscribe To This Newsgroup from the menu that appears, as shown below.

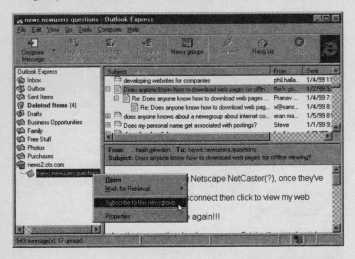

▶ If you're in the Newsgroups dialog box, click the name of the newsgroup you're interested in and then click the Subscribe button.

Once you've subscribed to a newsgroup, its name appears beneath the newsgroup server name in the folders list of Outlook Express. It's no longer "dimmed," as it may have looked after choosing the Go To button earlier. If you don't see subscribed newsgroups listed under the name of your news server in the folder list, click the + sign next to the news server name to expand the list. Figure 9.7 shows an example where I've subscribed to four newsgroups.

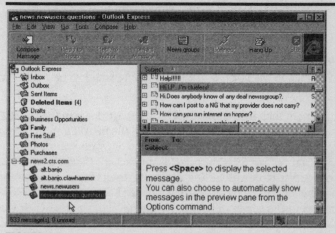

FIGURE 9.7: Four newsgroups I've subscribed to listed under news2.cts.com in the folders list

Be aware that if you "Go To" a newsgroup, but don't subscribe to it, its icon in the folders list will be dimmed. When you exit Outlook Express, the unsubscribed newsgroups will automatically be removed from the folders list.

TIP

To unsubscribe from a newsgroup, right-click its name in the folder list and choose Unsubscribe From This Newsgroup.

Browsing Newsgroup Articles

Once you've subscribed to one or more newsgroups, you'll probably want to start digging a little deeper into its articles and conversation threads. To get started:

1. Open Outlook Express (if it isn't open already).

2. If there is a + sign next to the name of your news server in the folder list, click that + sign to view the newsgroups you've subscribed to.

3. Beneath the name of your news server in the folder list, click the newsgroup whose message you want to view. The top pane will list all the articles in the group.

4. Click any article header in the top pane to view its contents in the bottom pane, just as you would when reading your e-mail.

You can then read the body of the message down in the preview pane. If instead of the message, you see the instruction to "Press <Space>..." and if pressing the space bar only gets you an instruction that reads, "This message is not cached. Please connect to your server to download the message," then the message is not on your local PC and can't be downloaded because you're not connected to the server anymore. No biggie, though. Just click the Connect button in the toolbar. Outlook Express will re-connect to your news server. Once you're connected, you can then right-click the message header in the top pane and choose Download This Message from the menu that appears.

TIP

A torn-page icon to the left of a header indicates that only the message header has been downloaded to your PC. A full-page icon to the left of the header means that the both the header and message body have already been downloaded to your PC.

Replying to a Message

As you read messages, you may come across one or more that you want to reply to. For example, perhaps a person is asking the group a question, and you happen to know the answer to that question. There are two ways you can send a reply:

▶ To reply to the group, so that everyone in the newsgroup can see your reply, click the Reply To Group button on the Outlook Express toolbar.

▶ To reply privately to the author of the article, so that only he or she can see your response, click the Reply To Author button.

Either way, a window will pop up allowing you to type your response. This window is exactly the same one you use to compose e-mail messages. However, the To: and Subject parts of the message are already filled in. Don't change them! Type your reply above the Original Message and click the Send button just above and to the left of the To: box. Simple.

Posting New Messages

As a beginner, you may spend more time asking questions than answering them. To ask the group a question, you need to post an article to the newsgroup. Here's how:

1. In the folder list, click the newsgroup to which you want to send a message.

2. Click the Compose Message button on the Outlook Express toolbar. The New Message window opens, pre-addressed to the newsgroup you selected in Step 1.

3. In the Subject box, type a brief subject that describes your post.

NEWSGROUP NETIQUETTE

The rules of etiquette that apply to e-mail also apply to newsgroups. When typing your message, don't use ALL UPPERCASE LETTERS. Don't post ads or anything that looks like an ad. Never leave the Subject line blank.

Furthermore, if you're replying to a post, don't change the Subject line at all. A conversation thread is really no more than a series of messages with the same Subject line. If you change the Subject line, your message will be treated as a new article and won't look like a reply to an existing message.

4. In the larger area of the window, type your message. Figure 9.8 shows an example where I'm about to post some questions to the `news.newusers.questions` newsgroup.

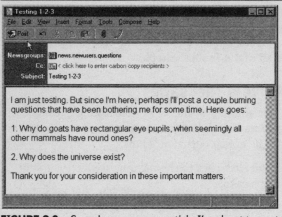

FIGURE 9.8: Sample newsgroup article I'm about to post to `news.newusers.questions`

5. When you've finished typing your message, click the Post button near the upper left corner of the dialog box.

The message will either be posted to the newsgroup immediately or just sent to your outbox. It all depends on the "Send messages immediately," described in the previous chapter. If the message just goes to your outbox, you'll need to choose Tools ➢ Send from the Outlook Express menu bar to actually post the message to the newsgroup.

You'll see a "Posting messages..." dialog box and a progress indicator as the article is posted. (If you have any unsent e-mail messages in your Outbox, those will be sent before the newsgroup article is posted.) When the post is complete, you're done. Your article is now travelling around the world and landing in thousands of ISP's news servers.

View Your Own Post

It should only take a few minutes for your message to be posted to the newsgroup. Though it may not appear in your message list because your list of header messages represents items that were in that newsgroup the moment you performed the download. But if you just wait a couple minutes you should be able to spot your own message by re-downloading new messages from the group. Here's how:

1. In the Outlook Express folder list, click the name of the newsgroup to which you posted the message.

2. From the Outlook Express menu bar choose Tools ➤ Download This Newsgroup.

3. In the Download Newsgroup dialog box that appears, choose Get The Following Items.

4. Choose New Headers (if you just want to download message headers) or New Messages (headers and bodies) if you want new messages and the message bodies (which will take a little longer).

5. Click the OK button in the Download Newsgroup dialog box.

If you've waited long enough for your message to get to your news server, you should see it somewhere in the list of message headers. In Figure 9.9, I've located the message I posted back in the preceding section of this chapter.

If you can't find your message in the list of headers because the list is too long, sort the messages by date so they're in chronological order. To do that, just click the Sent column heading in the headers list.

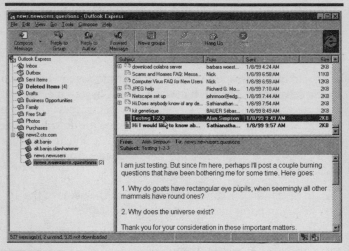

FIGURE 9.9: My message has been posted to the news group

NOTE

When you click a column heading in the headers list, all messages are sorted in ascending order by the column. The second time you click that same column head, the messages are sorted in descending order. So new messages will either be at the top or the bottom of the message list depending on whether they're currently sorted in ascending (oldest to newest) or descending (newest to oldest) order.

TIP

You can also search the message list for a name or subject. Click anywhere in the list of message headers and then choose Edit ➢ Find Message. In the dialog box that appears, type any part of your name or any part of the message subject. For example, I could type *Alan* to locate messages from myself. Then click the Find button. If the first matching message isn't the one you were looking for, choose Edit ➢ Find Next or press F3.

One way or another, you should be able to find your message. Don't expect any immediate replies though. It might take a day or two before someone who knows the answer to your question sees your message and sends a reply.

Checking for Replies

So let's say a day or two passes and you want to see if anyone has answered your profound question. Basically, all you need to do is fire up Outlook Express, go to the appropriate newsgroup again, and take a peek. Here are the steps:

1. Start Outlook Express in the usual manner. If prompted to connect, go ahead and do so.

2. In the folders list, click the + sign next to the name of your news server. Then click the name of the newsgroup to which you posted your question.

3. To bring your message list up to date, choose Tools ➢ Download This Newsgroup. Then choose Get The Following Items ➢ New Headers (or New Messages) and click the OK button.

4. When the new messages have been downloaded, choose View ➢ Current View ➢ Replies To My Post.

The list of message headers will shrink dramatically, displaying only messages that are direct replies to your post. (If there are no replies, the top panel will be empty.) To view the body of any reply, click its header in the top pane. In Figure 9.10, I'm viewing a reply to the message I posted earlier.

NOTE

OK, so I replied to my own post to create Figure 9.10. I know that wouldn't make sense in the real world, but I didn't want to wait around to see if anyone would really reply.

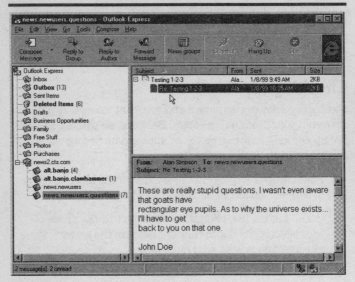

FIGURE 9.10: A reply to my message

After checking your replies, don't forget to choose View ➤ Current Replies ➤ All Messages to display all the message headers again.

And that, in a nutshell, is how newsgroups work. You post your message, then check back for replies once in a while.

Newsgroup Help

Don't forget that Outlook Express has its own built-in help, which you can use to supplement information provided in this chapter. As with most Windows programs, you just have to choose Help ➤ Contents And Index from the Outlook Express menu bar to get help. When the Outlook Express Help window appears, click the Contents tab and then click *Viewing and Posting to Newsgroups*. The tips and tricks and troubleshooting books also offer some solutions for newsgroupies.

Accessing Newsgroups via the Web

There are a couple of services on the World Wide Web that allow you access to newsgroups via your Web browser. If your ISP doesn't offer a news server, the Web is really your only choice for accessing newsgroups. But even if you do have access to a news server, the Web sites for newsgroups can be a great way to scan multiple newsgroups for topics of interest to you and for answers to burning questions. The two main Web sites that offer access to newsgroups are:

▶ http://www.dejanews.com

▶ http://www.liszt.com/news

You can visit either newsgroup just by typing its URL in Internet Explorer's Address bar.

Here's how the newsgroup Web sites work. Let's say you go to www.dejanews.com. On the first page you should find a Search box that allows you to look up any word or phrase. Let's say you're thinking of adopting a pet chinchilla and you want to find newsgroups and articles dealing with chinchillas. You'd just type the appropriate phrase into the search box, as shown below, and then click the Find button.

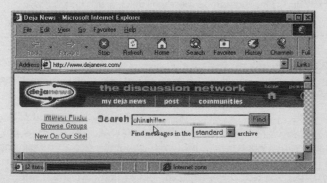

After a brief delay, a list of messages dealing with that subject appears, as shown in Figure 9.11. If you use Outlook Express as your

newsreader, you might just want to make note of the newsgroup names in the fourth column and then go back to Outlook Express and see if you can find that news group on your ISP's news server.

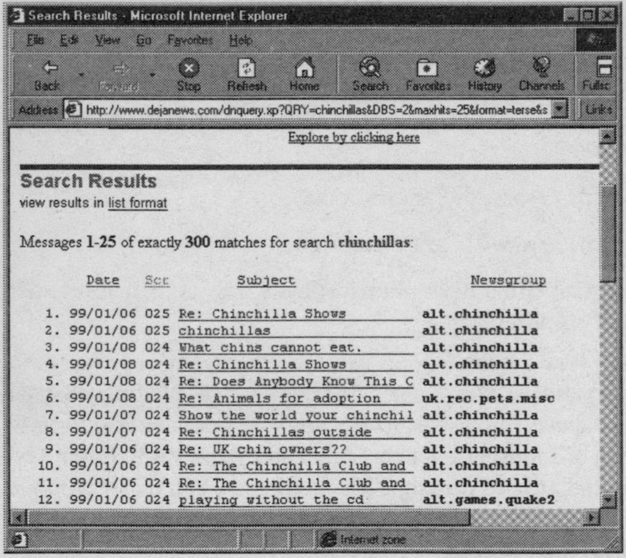

FIGURE 9.11:   Newsgroup messages dealing with chinchillas

You can also access messages and even post replies right from your Web browser. To view a message, you can click any blue, underlined link to view any message in the list. When you're viewing a message, you'll see additional options such as View Thread and Post Reply, as shown in the example shown in Figure 9.12.

Keep in mind that the people who create Web pages can change those pages at any time. So the instructions I just gave you could be outdated when you get around to using the Web for newsgroups. I hope that won't happen. But if it does, and the new page has instructions that differ from the ones I just gave you, then by all means follow those newer instructions on the page.

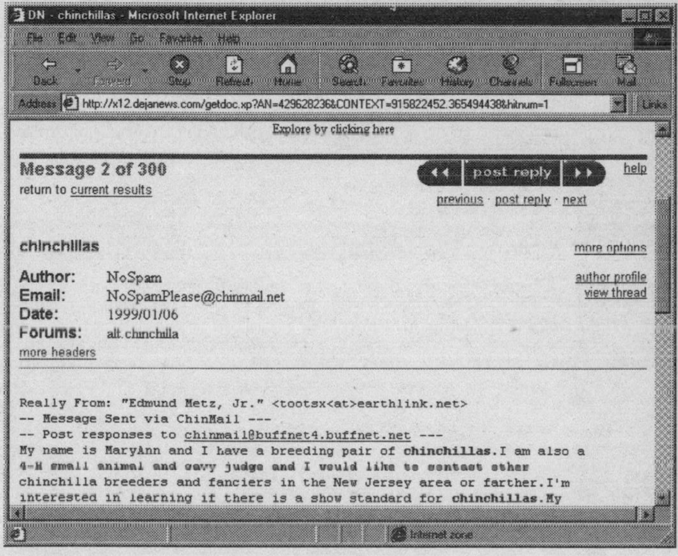

FIGURE 9.12: Viewing a newsgroup message via dejanews.com

Mailing Lists

Mailing lists are similar to newsgroups, only they use regular e-mail rather than a news server and news reader. There are mailing lists on just about every topic imaginable—you just have to find ones that interest you. But that's not too hard to do because the Liszt Mailing List Directory keeps track of tens of thousands of mailing lists. To get to that Web site, point your Web browser, Microsoft Internet Explorer, to http://www.liszt.com.

The first page should provide a text box and "go" button that you can use to search for lists on your favorite topic. For example, if I search Liszt for mailing lists on *baseball*, I find that there are quite a few mailing lists out there having to do with baseball, as shown in Figure 9.13.

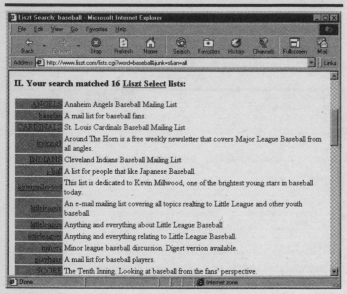

FIGURE 9.13: Mailing lists that discuss baseball

To learn more about a mailing list, click its link. The next page to appear will give you more information on that list. Most mailing lists originate from a Web site, and the information page that appears will provide a link to that site. Just click the link to go to the site, where you can learn more how to subscribe to the mailing list. Others might just offer an e-mail address. You can click that link, type up a message saying you're interested in learning more about the mailing list, and send it off.

Once you've subscribed to a mailing list, you'll get e-mail messages daily or weekly (or whatever, depending on the mailing list) from that site. These will arrive in your regular e-mail Inbox, just like any normal e-mail message. Just open the message as you would any regular e-mail.

Since different mailing lists have different rules and different ways of unsubscribing, I can't really tell you how to work a particular mailing list. However, most lists will come with all the instructions you need to use that mailing list effectively.

Good Things to Remember

So that about wraps it up for newsgroups and mailing lists. In the next chapter, you'll learn another way to communicate with people via the Web—live chatting. First, the customary chapter review:

► Usenet newsgroups are discussion groups where people who share similar interests can discuss things and get answers to questions.

► If your ISP offers a news (NNTP) server, you can use Outlook Express to connect to that server and view and post messages.

► After you set up Outlook Express to connect to your news server, the name of that server will appear in the Outlook Express folder list.

► To do anything with newsgroups, you first want to click the news server's name in the Outlook Express folder list.

► Subscribed newsgroups appear as icons under the newsgroup's name in the folders list.

► If your ISP doesn't offer newsgroups or if you ever want to search multiple newsgroups for certain kinds of information, you can visit one of the discussion-related Web sites such as www.dejanews.com or www.liszt.com/news.

► Mailing lists are another approach to allowing people with similar interests to communicate. To explore available mailing lists, stop by www.liszt.com on the Web.

Chapter 10

YACKITY YACK, LET'S CHAT

C hatting is yet another way of communicating with people on the Internet. Unlike e-mail and newsgroups, which involve sending messages, chatting is more like a real-time back-and-forth conversation between two people. Only you don't talk: You type messages back and forth. Technically, the protocol for chatting is called IRC—for Internet Relay Chat—which I mention only because you might stumble across that acronym from time to time. Normal people just call it "chatting."

Introducing Microsoft Chat

The freebie program that comes with Windows that you'll use to chat on the Internet is called Microsoft Chat. To open that program:

1. Click the Windows Start button.

2. Choose Programs ➣ Internet Explorer ➣ Microsoft Chat.

If Microsoft Chat isn't already installed on your PC, you can install it using the Windows Setup tab in Add/Remove Programs or, you can download a copy from Microsoft's Web site at

▶ http://www/microsoft.com/windows/ie/chat

or

▶ http://www/microsoft.com/msdownload

Define Yourself

When you first start Microsoft Chat, you'll be taken to the Connect tab of the Chat Connection dialog box. There you can choose a *chat server* and a *chat room*. As a newbie, you'll want to start at the suggested server and room shown below.

On the Personal Info tab, fill in as much, or as little, about your-self as you care to make public. All the fields are optional so you can leave them blank if you wish (or fill the fields with false infor-mation if you just want to have some fun).

On the Character tab, choose a character to represent yourself. Just click each name until you find a character you like. Below, I chose Lance.

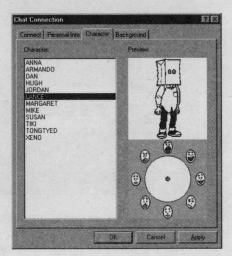

TIP

To change your identity at any time, choose View ➤ Options from Chat's menu bar and make selections from the Personal Info and Character tabs.

On the Background tab, choose whichever background you like. When you've finished making your selections, click the OK button. At that point your PC will connect to the Internet (or ask you to connect to the Internet). Go ahead and do so.

Once you're connected to the chat server, you might see a Message Of The Day dialog box. You can decide for yourself whether you want to read that message. Then click its OK button to get into the Chat program.

TIP

If nothing seems to work in Chat, you may be offline. In that case, the message *Now working offline* will appear in the status bar. To get back online, click the Connect button in the toolbar or choose File ➢ New Connection and then click OK.

Finding a Chat Room

Most chat servers are divided into *rooms* where people who share a similar interest meet and chat. To see what rooms are available on your chat server, choose Room ➢ Room List from Chat's menu bar. The Chat Room List dialog box shown in Figure 10.1 appears.

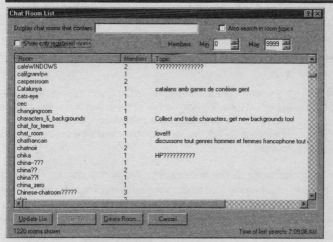

FIGURE 10.1: The Chat Room List dialog box

You can scroll through the list to see if you can find something that interests you or...

▶ To see which rooms are most/least crowded, click the Members column heading once to arrange them from least-to-most crowded and click again to arrange from most-to-least crowded.

▶ To search for a specific topic, type a word into the *Display chat rooms that contain* text box and select the check box to the right of that option. The list will narrow to rooms that contain that word (if any). To return to the complete list, delete text from the *Display chat rooms that contain* box.

To join a room:

1. Click the name of the room you want to join.

2. Click the Go To button.

You may see some automatic messages appear on the screen describing the rules of the chat room. Then you'll see ongoing conversations between room members appearing as comics. The members list in the top right pane lists all the members of the current chat room. To see a list without the character faces, right-click that pane and choose List.

TIP

If you don't see comic frames in Chat, you're probably working in text view. To switch between comic and text views, choose View from the menu bar, then either Comic Strip or Plain Text. Alternatively, click the Comics View or Text View button in Chat's toolbar.

Each character in the comics represents one chatter. To see a character's nickname, just hover your mouse pointer over any character in any comic. The nickname appears in a tiny box near the mouse pointer. To see a chatter's profile, right-click the character and choose Get Profile. A series of frames appears, showing that person's personal information.

Join In the Conversation

To join in the conversation, you need to start chatting. Here's how (though, you can do steps 1–3 in any order you wish):

1. Type whatever you want to say in the strip near the bottom of the dialog box.

2. If you want your character to show an emotion, drag the little black ball in the emotion wheel, shown below, until your character shows the expression you want.

3. If you want to direct your message to a specific character, click that character in any comic frame or in the members list.

4. Click the Say button or any of the other buttons as summarized in Table 10.1. Alternatively, you can press the shortcut key listed in the third column if you don't want to take your hands off the keyboard.

TABLE 10.1: Chat buttons for displaying your text

Button	Name	What it Does
	Say	Puts your message on the screen in a talk bubble (Ctrl+Y)
	Think	Puts your message on the screen in a thought bubble (Ctrl+T)
	Whisper	"Whispers" your message to only the character you selected in Step 2 above (Ctrl+W)
	Action	Displays your message as a caption rather than in a bubble (Ctrl+A)

That, in a nutshell, is what chatting is all about. You type a message and send it along. It appears on your screen and all the other room members' screens almost instantly. (Unless you whisper to someone, in which case your message appears only on that person's screen and your own.) As you may have guessed, though, there are plenty of options to play around with in Chat, as I'll discuss next.

CHAT ACRONYMS

Many of the acronyms that appear in your e-mail messages and newsgroup articles will show up in chats as well. Some favorites among chatters include:

A/S/L Age / Sex / Location

AFK Away from keyboard

BRB Be right back

CYA See ya

EAK Eating at keyboard

K Okay

LOL Laughing out loud

NP No problem

TY Thank you

ROTFL Rolling on the floor laughing

WB Welcome back

Whisper in my Ear

The Whisper button lets you send a single, private message to a member. If you'd like to have a lengthy private conversation with a member, you can sneak off to the whisper box. There, you and one or more other people can send messages back and forth without others seeing your messages. If you'd like to initiate a private conversation:

1. Type a message in the bottom line, as usual.

2. In the room member list, click the member you want to whisper to.

3. Alternatively, to whisper to several members, hold down the Ctrl key as you click their names in the members list.

4. Choose Member ➤ Whisper Box from Chat's menu bar. You're taken to the Whisper Box, which looks something like Figure 10.2.

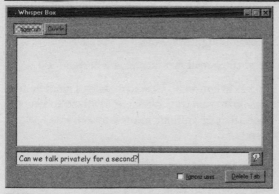

FIGURE 10.2: Chat's whisper box

5. Type your message in the long text box and click the Whisper button to send it.

If someone initiates a private conversation with you, you'll see the whisper box with that person's message in it. You can join in the private conversation simply by typing your reply in the bottom line and clicking the Whisper button to the right. If you don't want to join in, just close the Whisper box. If the whisperer is insistent, and you want to get rid of them, you can click the Ignore User checkbox before you close the Whisper box. You won't get any more whispers from that member.

Sending E-mail to a Member

You can also communicate privately with a member by sending them an e-mail—provided that member has included his or her e-mail address in their personal information. To send an e-mail message:

1. Right-click the member's character in the comic pane or the member list.

2. Choose Send E-mail. Outlook Express (or your default e-mail program) will open with a New Message window, with the chat member's e-mail address already filled in.

3. Type in a subject and message and then press Send.

4. Type and send the e-mail message as you normally do.

If Outlook Express is not set up to send messages immediately, the message will just go to your Outlook Express outbox. To send the message, you'll need to open Outlook Express and choose Tools ➤ Send from its menu bar.

Sending and Receiving Files

You can also send any file on your PC to a member. In the member list, right-click the name of member you want to send a file to and choose Send File. In the Send File dialog box that appears, browse to and click the file you want to send. Then click the Open button. You'll see a message indicating that Chat is waiting for the other person to accept the file. If they do, the file will be sent.

If someone sends you a file, you'll see a message asking if you want to accept the file. But be careful—some files can contain viruses and other unpleasant things that are not good for your PC. Don't accept the file unless you feel confident you know what you're getting.

Browsing Rooms

You may want to hop around from room to room until you find one you really like. Here's how you can do that:

1. To leave the room you're in right now, choose Room ➤ Leave Room from Chat's menu bar (or click the Leave Room button in the toolbar).

2. To find a new room, choose Room ➤ Room List (or click the Chat Room List button in the toolbar).

You'll be returned to the room list where you can dig around for other rooms. To enter a new room, click whichever room you want to join and then click the Go To button.

Logging Off

When you've finished your chat session, don't forget to disconnect from the server. If you want to announce your exit first, click the Leave Room button in the toolbar. To disconnect, click the Disconnect button in the toolbar. Then exit chat by clicking its Close (X) button or by choosing File ➤ Exit from its menu bar.

More on Microsoft Chat

If you become a Chat fan, there are some more resources on the Internet you might want to check out. Here are a couple of Chat-related Web sites you can visit with Internet Explorer:

- ▶ Microsoft Chat's Page at `http://www.microsoft.com/windows/ie/chat`

- ▶ MSN Web Communities at `http://communities.msn.com`

- ▶ Frequently-Asked Questions at `http://communities.msn.com/chat/faq.asp`

▶ Code of Conduct at `http://communities.msn.com/chat/conduct.asp`

▶ Unofficial Chat Page `http://members.tripod.com/ComicChat`.

Good Things to Remember

Chatting is a fun way to meet people online and share in some light banter. It's also the easiest Internet feature to use, which makes for a nice short chapter! Key points to remember:

▶ When you want to chat online, just fire up your Microsoft Chat program (Start ➤ Programs ➤ Internet Explorer ➤ Chat).

▶ While you're in Chat, choose View ➤ Options to choose your chat character or change your personal information.

▶ To see all the rooms available on the current chat server, choose Room ➤ Room List from Chat's menu bar. To enter a room, click its name and then click the Go To button.

▶ To chat, type your message in the bottom line.

▶ Use the emotion wheel to give your character an emotion.

▶ To send your message to a particular member, click that member's name in the name list or character in the comic panes.

▶ Click the Say, Think, or Whisper button to the right of where you typed you text.

▶ If you get disconnected from the chat server, choose File ➤ New Connection from Chat's menu bar.

Chapter 11

MEET ME ONLINE

I n this chapter, you'll learn about Internet conferencing, where
you can hold meetings with people all over the world. During
these meetings you can chat as well as speak by voice, view one
another by video, send and receive files, share programs, and share
an electronic whiteboard. The computers on the Internet that support conferencing are called *directory servers* or *ILS servers* (where
ILS stands for Internet Locator Service). The program you'll use
on your PC to conference is named Microsoft NetMeeting.

Introducing Microsoft NetMeeting

Microsoft NetMeeting supports both sound and video but only if
you have the appropriate hardware installed on your PC. For example, if you want to be able to talk over the Internet, your PC needs
to have a sound card, speakers, and a microphone. If you want to
show your face via video, your PC needs to have some kind of video-
camera device attached. If you don't have those items, you can still
use NetMeeting to participate in a conference. You just won't be
able to use the voice or video features.

To start Microsoft NetMeeting, follow these simple steps:

1. Click the Windows Start button.

2. Choose Programs ≻ Internet Explorer ≻ Microsoft
NetMeeting.

If you can't find NetMeeting, chances are it has never been
installed. You can install it via the Windows Setup tab in Add/
Remove Programs, as discussed under "Installing Missing Windows Components" in Appendix B. Optionally, you can also download a copy from Microsoft's download site at `http://www`
`.microsoft.com/netmeeting`.

The first time you start NetMeeting on your PC, a Wizard titled
Microsoft NetMeeting appears on your screen. Getting through
the Wizard is pretty easy:

1. After reading the first Wizard screen, click the Next
button.

TIP
The Wizard only appears the first time you start NetMeeting. If it doesn't start on your PC, don't worry about it. You can do everything that needs to be done inside the NetMeeting program by choosing Tools ➢ Options from NetMeeting's menu bar.

2. On the second Wizard screen, choose a directory server from the drop-down list, as in the example shown in Figure 11.1. Then click the Next button.

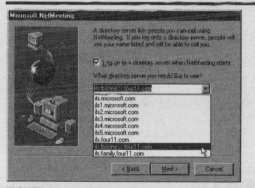

FIGURE 11.1: Choosing a directory server from the Netmeeting Wizard

3. On the third Wizard screen, fill in your first and last name and e-mail address. The other fields on that page are optional—you can leave them blank if you prefer. Click the Next button when done.

4. On the fourth Wizard screen, you need to identify your reasons for using NetMeeting as either Business, Personal, or Adults Only. Other people will see this selection when you're added to the directory list and will (hopefully) respect it. For example, you might want to choose the "For personal use (suitable for all ages)," which will hopefully keep the raunchier members from sending unsuitable messages via NetMeeting.

5. On the fifth Wizard screen choose whichever option best describes your connection. (If you have a 56K modem, choose the 28800 bps or Faster Modem option.) Then click the Next button.

6. The next Wizard screen helps you fine-tune your audio settings, provided you have a microphone connected to your PC. Click the Next button and follow the instructions on the screen. If you don't have a microphone, don't worry about it. Also, don't worry about getting everything just perfect. You can easily readjust your audio settings at any time in the future.

7. When you get to the last Wizard screen, click the Finish button. If your computer isn't set up to dial in automatically when NetMeeting starts, you'll be prompted to connect. Go ahead and do so.

You may see a message indicating that there was a problem logging onto the server you chose back in step 2. Choose OK to clear that message to get to NetMeeting's main screen, shown in Figure 11.2.

Are You Logged On?

Before you do anything else in NetMeeting, take a look at the "logged on" indicator in the status bar, pointed out in Figure 11.2. One of the following messages will appear:

▶ If the message says "Logged in to *some server name,*" then skip to the section titled "NetMeeting's Directory List."

▶ If the indicator says "Not logged on," then continue reading below.

Getting logged on to a directory server is a real challenge these days. There are not enough servers right now to accommodate all the people wanting to use them. Because the Internet is such a new technology, technical problems can occur with servers, ISPs, and such that make it hard to connect, particularly with dial-up accounts.

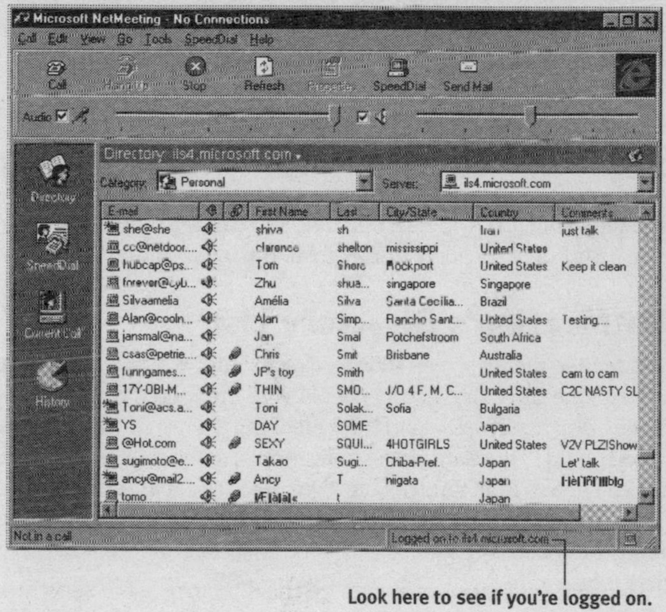

Look here to see if you're logged on.

FIGURE 11.2: NetMeeting's main screen and important status bar indicator.

You really can't do anything in NetMeeting until you're logged on to a server, so you need to keep trying. To attempt a log on to a different server, follow these steps:

1. Choose Tools ➢ Options from NetMeeting's menu bar.

2. Click the Calling tab.

3. Choose a different server name from the Server Name drop-down list.

4. Click the OK button.

5. If you see a message indicating that you're not logged into a server, you can say "Duh" (since that's the reason you did steps 1–4) and then click the OK button.

The status bar indicator will read "Logging on to *some server name*" as NetMeeting attempts to log on. If successful, the indicator quietly changes to "Logged on to *some server name,*" and you're in business. You can move on to the next section.

If you end up with a message saying you can't get on and the status bar indicator shows "Not logged on," then you'll have to repeat steps 1–5 to try yet another server. You may have to try several servers before you find one that you can log on to. (It can be very irritating, especially during peak business hours!)

NetMeeting's Directory List

NetMeeting's main screen shows a *directory list,* which is sort of like a telephone directory, listing people who are logged onto various servers. You might see some strange-looking characters in there, like |^Å||_ç_||. Those are not an indication of some problem. They're just characters from foreign languages, such as Japanese, that have no equivalent in English and end up looking they way they do. So don't worry about those.

There are several ways to explore the directory list to see who's logged into a server or to find a specific person that you're trying to contact:

▶ To limit the list to a specific category, such as Business users, choose the category from the Category drop-down list, as shown below.

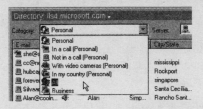

▶ To sort the list by any column, click the button above the column you want to use for sorting. For example, click the Last Name button to sort names by last name. Clicking the same button again reverses the order of the sort.

▶ To widen or narrow columns, drag the line that separates the column headings to the left or right. Double-click a column heading to return it to its default size.

▶ You can also rearrange the columns by dragging any column heading to the left or right.

Directory List Icons

Icons listed in the left columns of the directory listing tell you a little about each person in the list, as summarized in Table 11.1.

TABLE 11.1: Icons in NetMeeting's directory list

ICON	WHAT IT MEANS
	This person is available for calling.
	This person is currently in a call.
	This person has audio capabilities.
	This person has the ability to send video.

Finding Your Name

Once you're logged onto a server, you should be able to find your own name in the directory list. For example, if you sort the list by the Last Name column and then scroll down to the first letter of your last name, you should find your name listed in the directory. If you do not see your name listed, do the following:

▶ Make sure you're viewing the directory list. Click the Directory button in the navigation list at the left side of NetMeeting's window or choose View ➤ Directory from the NetMeeting's menu bar.

▶ Make sure the name of the server that appears in the Server drop-down list matches the name of the server that you're logged onto, as pointed out in Figure 11.3.

▶ Make sure the Category drop-down list matches the category you put yourself in (or is displaying All members), as indicated in Figure 11.3.

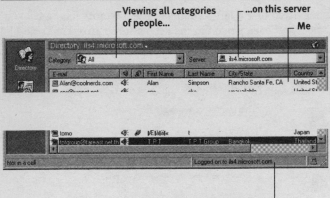

Viewing all categories of people...

...on this server

Me

Same server I'm logged on to

FIGURE 11.3:   Your name will show up only when the server names and categories match.

▶ If you still don't see your own name, follow the steps below to make sure you aren't hidden from the directory list:

   1. Choose Tools ➤ Options from NetMeeting's menu bar and then click the Calling tab in the dialog box that appears.

   2. Be sure the second checkbox, Do Not List My Name..., is unselected (does not contain a checkmark).

   3. Click the OK button.

▶ Finally, click the Refresh button in NetMeeting's toolbar or press the F5 key to bring the directory list up-to-date.

You can visit other servers and view the directory listing of people logged on to the those servers using the Server drop-down list at the top of the directory list. You can also contact anyone in any of those lists. Remember that your name will only show up when the server you select matches the name of the server you're logged on to. The status bar indicator will always show the name of the server you're actually logged on to.

Call Someone

To communicate with someone on a directory server, you need to place a call to that person. You can do this by following these steps:

1. In the directory list, click the name of the person you wish to call.

2. Click the Call button in NetMeeting's toolbar. You'll be taken to the New Call dialog box. If you were placing a call to me and I happened to be logged onto ils4 .microsoft.com, the New Call dialog box would look like this:

3. Click the Call button in the dialog box and then wait.

If the other person answers, NetMeeting's directory list changes to a Current Call list showing only the names of the people involved in the current call. If the person you called doesn't answer, you'll see a message on the screen indicating that the person isn't accepting the call. You'll be given the option to send them an e-mail message instead.

If the other person does accept the call, NetMeeting's directory list changes to a Current Call list, showing only you and the person with whom you have called. Figure 11.4 shows an example of the Current Call list where two people are connected. One of them has a video camera attached, and you can see that geeky guy in the figure.

FIGURE 11.4: The Current Call list with two people connected in a call

TIP

If you want to add more people to the current call, click the Directory button in the left column and then repeat the steps above to call the other person. To return to the Current Call list at any time, just click the Current Call button in the left column.

People in the current call list are connected to one another, which means they can talk (if they have audio capabilities), view each other on video (if they have video), transfer files, use the whiteboard, and share applications, as discussed in the sections that follow.

HOW MANY PEOPLE?

You can call up to 32 people to collaborate in a Net-Meeting conference. All those members can chat, use the Whiteboard, and send files to one another. However, a maximum of three people in the meeting can access shared applications simultaneously. Only two of those members can communicate by voice or video at a time. As discussed later in this chapter, it's easy to switch between members while using voice or video. You can still conference by voice or video with several people.

Receiving a Call

If somebody calls you for a NetMeeting conference, your computer will ring (if you have a sound card), and you'll see a message on the screen indicating who placed the call. To accept the call, click the Accept button in that dialog box. You'll be put into the Current Call list shown in Figure 11.4. If you prefer to reject the call, click the Ignore button.

TIP

If you want to stay logged on to your directory server, but don't want to be bothered by incoming calls, choose Call ≻ Do Not Disturb from NetMeeting's menu bar. You won't get any more incoming calls until you choose Call ≻ Do Not Disturb again to disable that feature.

Chatting in NetMeeting

Chatting in NetMeeting is similar to chatting with Microsoft Chat. You type messages back and forth. To do so, follow these steps:

1. Make sure you're in the current Call list (click the Current Call button in the left column).

2. Click the Chat button in NetMeeting's toolbar or choose Tools ≻ Chat from NetMeeting's menu bar. The Chat window opens and shows how many people in the current call are using the same chat window.

3. To send a message, just type in the lower Message area whatever you want to say. If you have trouble typing, click anywhere in the box labeled Message to put the blinking cursor in that box first.

4. When you finished typing your message, you can click the large button to the right of the Message box or press Enter. Alternatively, to whisper your message to a single participant, choose that person's name from the Send To drop-down list before you click the large button.

Figure 11.5 shows a sample chat in progress. When you've finished chatting you can close the chat window by clicking the Close (X) button in the upper right corner of the chat window. You'll be asked if you want to save the current session. If you would like to keep a record of the session, choose Yes, then pick a folder, and enter a filename for storing the session. The chat text will be saved in a standard text file, which you can later open with any text editor, including the Notepad and WordPad programs that come with Windows.

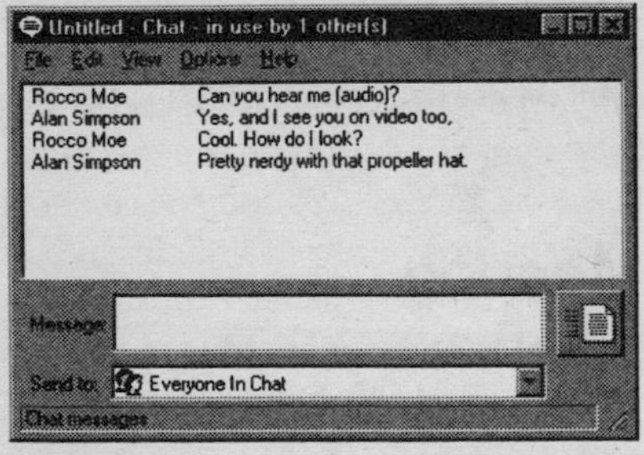

FIGURE 11.5: Sample NetMeeting chat in progress

Talking on the Internet

If you and some other person in the current call both have a sound card, speakers, and a microphone, you can talk rather than type messages back and forth. Once you're in a call, the audio capabilities should turn on automatically. All you have to do is start talking into your microphone.

TIP

Your voice is carried over the Internet, not over traditional phone lines. Ma Bell will never know, and there will be nothing on your phone bill related to the conversation. Even if you yack for an hours to someone halfway around the world!

There is one potential problem you need to be aware of. Sound cards come in two flavors—half-duplex and full-duplex. If your sound card supports full-duplex, you can use your microphone and speakers at the same time like a regular telephone. But if your sound card is half-duplex, sound can only travel in one direction at a time. So you need to take turns talking, like with a walkie-talkie or an older-style speaker phone. If your sound card is full-duplex, but is acting like it's half-duplex, choose Tools ➤ Options from NetMeeting's menu bar. In the dialog box that appears, click the Audio tab and select the Enable Full Duplex Audio... option. Then click the OK button.

If you have any problems with audio, you can use Chat to type messages back and forth while trying to resolve those problems. Chat and audio will work at the same time. You can use the audio toolbar shown below to adjust your microphone and speaker volume. If that toolbar isn't visible, choose View ➤ Toolbar from NetMeeting's menu bar. Also, make sure that the checkboxes next to the microphone and speaker are selected (checked) as below.

By the way, if you want to mute your microphone so nobody can hear you talk, clear the checkbox next to the microphone in that toolbar. If you want to mute your speakers so you can't hear others talk, clear the checkbox next to the speaker icon in that toolbar.

WARNING

If your microphone is too close to your speakers, you might get feedback (loud, irritating noises). Try to keep some distance between the two. If you want to use the audio Wizard that was discussed earlier in this chapter to adjust you speaker and volume control, choose Audio Tuning Wizard from NetMeeting's menu bar.

Remember that you can converse with only one other person at a time. If there are three or more people involved in the current call, you can decide who you want to talk to by choosing Tools ➢ Switch Audio And Video from NetMeeting's menu bar. Choose which person you want to speak with next, and then start speaking. The little speaker icon next to person's name will darken to indicate which person you're currently talking to.

To end a spoken conversation with someone, click the speaker icon next to that person's name in the Current Call list, and choose Stop Using Audio and Video in the menu that appears. You'll still be connected to that person and can still chat with them, use the whiteboard and such. You just won't have voice contact with that person any more.

Video Conferencing

If you have a video camera attached to your PC, the person you're in a call with will be able to see you. If the other person has a video camera, you'll be able to see them as well. The video image appears at the right side of Current Call list. If the person you're in a call with can't see you, despite the fact that you have a camera, click the Play/Pause button at the lower left corner of the video image. The message "Sending" appears, as below, when your video image is being sent. Likewise, if you're having a bad hair day or just got

out of bed, you can stop sending video just by clicking that same
button. The "Sending" indicator changes to "Paused."

TIP

You don't need a full-on camcorder to video conference, just
one of those little plastic jobs that sits on top of your computer
monitor like the Intel Create and Share Camera Pack (www
.intel.com/createshare).

As with audio, you can only video conference with one person
at a time. If you have several people connected in the current call
and want to switch your video to someone else, choose Tools ➢
Switch Audio and Video. Then click on the name of the person
you want to talk with.

Don't expect TV-quality video in NetMeeting, particularly if
you're using a dial-up connection. The bandwidth for high-quality
video isn't available in the telephone system. You do, however, have
some control over the quality of the video you're receiving. Choose
Tools ➢ Options from NetMeeting's menu bar and then click the
Video tab to get to the options shown in Figure 11.6.

The Video Quality option lets you choose between smooth-motion
video with lower picture quality (Faster video) or jerkier motion with
high-quality images (Better quality). Other options let you control
whether video kicks in automatically or not and the size of the image
video image you're sending. Don't forget to click the OK button
when you've finished making your selections.

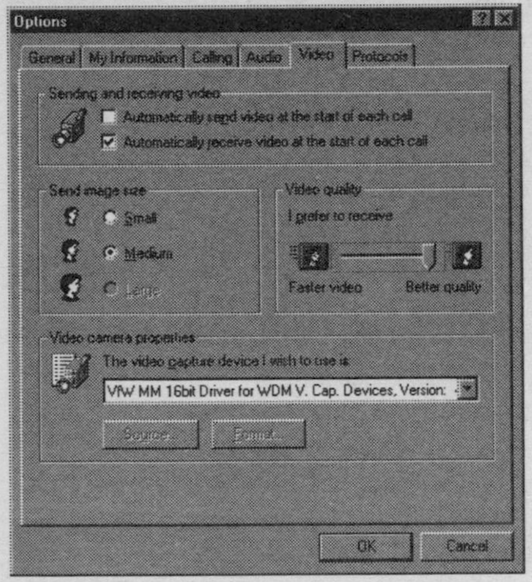

FIGURE 11.6: NetMeeting's video options

Video works best with computers that have a Pentium 133 MHz or faster chip in them. Even so, sharing applications and running a video at the same time can slow things down to a snail's pace. Pausing the video at such times should help speed things back up.

To stop sending audio a video to someone, click the speaker icon next to that person's name in the current call list and choose Stop Using Audio And Video in the menu that appears. You'll still be connected to that person and can still chat, send and receive files, use the Whiteboard, and so on.

Sending and Receiving Files

You can send a copy of any file on your computer to anybody in the current call. Just follow these steps:

1. In NetMeeting, make sure you're in the Current Call list.

2. Choose Tools ➢ File Transfer ➢ Send File from Net-Meeting's menu bar.

3. Browse to and click the name of the file you want to send.

4. Click the Send button.

You'll see a message indicating the file is being sent. Or, if it's a small file, you'll just see a message indicating that the file has been sent. While the file is being sent, every potential recipient of that file will see the dialog box allowing them to accept or receive the file. Once the transfer is complete, they're given the options shown below. Of course, if some sends you a file, you'll be given the same options.

The buttons in the dialog box let the recipient decide what to do with the sent file, as summarized below:

Close   Accepts the file without opening it.

Open   Accepts the file and displays it on the screen.

Delete   Rejects the sent file.

All files sent via NetMeeting are initially stored in the c:\Program Files\NetMeeting\Received Files folder. To see files sent to you and open them, choose Tools ➢ File Transfer ➢ Open Received Files Folder.

Sharing the Clipboard Contents

Everyone in NetMeeting also shares a common Windows Clipboard, which provides yet another way to easily share stuff. For instance, let's say you're viewing a photo in some graphics program. You click on that photo and press Ctrl+C or choose Edit ➤ Copy from the graphics program's menu bar. A copy of the picture is automatically sent to the Clipboard.

Now, suppose another member opens the same or a similar graphics program on their computer. If that person chooses Edit ➤ Paste from that program's menu bar (or presses Ctrl+V), the contents of *your* Windows clipboard will be pasted into *their* graphics program!

Using the Whiteboard

The Whiteboard is similar to Chat, but rather than typing messages back and forth, you draw pictures. The name "whiteboard" comes from its similarity to the big white drawing board often used in meetings. Everyone in the current call can see the whiteboard and draw on it as well. To open the whiteboard, click the Whiteboard button in NetMeeting's toolbar or choose Tools ➤ Whiteboard.

The Whiteboard pops up on your screen, as well as on the screen of everyone else in the current call. To draw on the Whiteboard, click any button in the left panel, such as the circle, to draw that shape. Then drag the mouse pointer around in the large area to make that shape. You can also type text using the Text (large letter *A*) button. Just play around with it as in Figure 11.7. You'll get the hang of it.

You can also copy a picture from any graphics program using the standard Windows Edit ➤ Copy or Ctrl+C method. Then choose Edit ➤ Paste to paste the image into the Whiteboard. Everyone in the current call will instantly see whatever image you paste into the Whiteboard.

FIGURE 11.7: The Whiteboard a picture and text

When you've finished with the Whiteboard, just click its Close (X) button to close it. You'll be given the option to save the contents of the Whiteboard. If you choose Yes, the file will be saved with a .wht (whiteboard) filename extension. In the future, you can reopen that same image by choosing File ➢ Open from the Whiteboard's menu bar.

The Whiteboard also has its own online help. If you need help while using the Whiteboard, choose Help ➢ Help Topics from its menu bar.

Sharing Applications

One of the coolest features of NetMeeting, though a little hard to get used to, is the ability to share applications. For instance, you can pop a Microsoft Word document on screen and have all members work on that application together. Here's how you do it:

1. Close any application programs that you don't want to share.

2. Open the document you want to share. You can also create a new document by opening whichever program is best suited to creating that type of application.

3. Make sure you're still in the current call list and then click the Share button in the toolbar or choose Tools ➤ Share Application from the menu bar. Then click the name of the application you want to share.

4. Initially, everyone will be able to see the document or program, but they won't be able to make any changes to it.

5. To allow others to make changes to the document, click the Collaborate button in NetMeeting's toolbar.

6. Click the OK button in the dialog box that appears.

Now, whatever you see on the screen while working on the document will be plainly visible to others in the meeting. For someone else to "take control" and put in their own two cents, all that person needs to do is click anywhere in the document and choose OK in the dialog box that appears.

Once that other person has control, you can just sit back and watch them do their thing. Everything they do appears on your screen. (Kind of like there's a ghost in the room doing your work for you.) Any changes that the person makes happen in the original document; that is, if you're the one who shared the document, the changes will actually take place in the document on your computer.

To regain control over the shared application, click the document on your screen again. To stop allowing others to work on the document, get back to NetMeeting and click the Collaborate button again. The document will still be visible to others, but they will no longer be allowed to make changes. To stop sharing altogether, click the Share button again and click the name of the document you want to stop sharing. The document will now be visible on your machine only.

To save the changes that others made to the document, go back to the shared application window and choose File ➤ Save from its menu bar or close the program and choose Yes when asked about saving the changes. If you want everyone in the current call to have a copy of the document, you can send a copy of the saved document to each member as described under "Sending and Receiving Files" earlier in this chapter.

Ending a Call

To end a meeting, click the Hang Up button in NetMeeting's toolbar. To log off from the directory server, choose File ➣ Log Off From *servername*.

More NetMeeting Resources

What you've learned here will keep you busy with NetMeeting for a long time. But if you're looking for more information or you have any problems, you can explore other places, including these, to get more details:

- ▶ NetMeeting's online Help provides help for all NetMeeting tools including the Whiteboard, chat, and so forth. Choose Help ➣ Help Topics from NetMeeting's menu bar to access its online help.

- ▶ Microsoft's NetMeeting Web site at www.microsoft.com/NetMeeting provides updates to the program and news.

- ▶ NetMeeting 101 discusses NetMeeting basics and offers solutions to common problems at www.meetingbywire.com/NetMeeting101.htm.

- ▶ NetMeeting Servers Worldwide are listed on the Web at www.netmeet.com.

- ▶ Intel's Connected PC Web site at www.connectedPC.com offers tips and products for online communications.

Good Things to Remember

NetMeeting is a tool for conferencing on the Internet. Two or more people can chat, talk, see one another on video, exchange files, draw on a common whiteboard, and collaborate on documents. Remember these key points:

- ▶ To use the audio features of NetMeeting, your PC needs a sound card (preferably of the full-duplex variety), speakers, and a microphone.

▶ Anyone can receive video in NetMeeting. To send video though, you'll need a video camera—the small PC type you buy at computer stores.

▶ To start NetMeeting, click the Windows Start button and choose Programs ➢ Internet Explorer ➢ Microsoft NetMeeting.

▶ Once you're in NetMeeting, check the status bar to make sure you're logged into a server. If not, choose Tools ➢ Options. Click the Calling tab, choose a Server name, and then click the OK button.

▶ Once you're logged onto a server, the directory list in Net-Meeting will list other people who are logged into that same server.

▶ You can use the server drop-down list in NetMeeting's main window to view people who are logged onto other servers.

▶ To call someone in NetMeeting, click their name in the directory list and then click the Call button.

▶ Once you place a call and the other person accepts, you're taken to the current call list, which shows only people who are connected in the current call.

▶ Audio and video capabilities usually click in automatically as soon as a connection is made.

▶ To chat with people in the current call, click the Chat button in NetMeeting's toolbar.

▶ To draw in NetMeeting, click the Whiteboard button in the Toolbar.

▶ To send files to other people in the current call, choose Tools ➢ File Transfers ➢ Send File.

▶ To share a document, so others can see it, open the document on your PC. Then click the Share button in Net-Meeting's toolbar.

▶ If you want others to be able to contribute to the shared document, click the Collaborate button on the toolbar.

Appendix A

PROGRAMS TO HELP WITH THE INTERNET

Windows and Microsoft Internet Explorer come with programs to use all the major features of the Internet. You can round out that collection with some of the programs listed in this appendix. All of these are shareware, which means you can download them from the Internet and try them out for a limited time before you decide whether to buy. The Web site addresses next to each program shows where you can go to learn more and download a shareware version of that program. If you prefer to browse around online and see reviews of the products listed, visit any of the Web sites listed under "Shareware Centers" near the end of this appendix.

Anti-Virus Programs

Viruses don't just happen. It takes a sophisticated (and somewhat psychotic) programmer to create a virus. So fortunately, viruses are pretty rare. In my 20+ years of heavy computer use, I've never once come across a virus. But once a virus gets into a file on the Internet, it infects all the PCs that download that file. So it doesn't hurt to have some anti-virus software on your computer to detect and weed out viruses before they do any damage to your PC. Here are some sources for anti-virus programs on the Internet:

Program	URL
Command F-PROT Shareware	www.commandcom.com
McAfee Anti-Virus	www.mcafee.com
Norton Anti-Virus	www.symantec.com
PC-cillian	www.checkit.com
ThunderByte Anti-Virus	www.novastor.com

TIP
McAfee Anti-Virus also ships with the Microsoft Plus! program for Windows 98.

ANTI-VIRUS HARDWARE

Some computers come with anti-virus hardware built right in. To enable or disable that feature, you need to adjust your computer's CMOS settings. The only way to get to those settings is to start (or reboot) your computer and watch the screen as the computer is booting up. When you see a message that says something like:

```
Press key to enter setup
```

you have a few seconds to press the *key* shown in that message to get to your CMOS settings. I really can't tell you what will happen next, because the program for adjusting CMOS settings varies from one PC to the next. But if your computer does have built-in anti-virus hardware, you shouldn't have any trouble finding the option that lets you turn that feature on and off.

E-Mail Anti-Spam

Spam is the term used to describe junk mail and other forms of Internet advertising. E-mail anti-Spam programs help weed out junk mail from your e-mail messages before you waste your time reading the message. You need to use these programs with great care, however. They will delete some e-mail messages before you ever see them. They need to be configured properly to avoid deleting useful messages! To learn about the crusade to end spamming, visit www.anti-spam.net.

Program	URL
CYBERSitter Anti-Spam	www.solidoak.com
MailTalkX	www.softbytelabs.com/MailTalkX
SpamEater Pro	www.hms.com/spameater.htm

Program	URL
SpamKiller	www.spamkiller.com
Spammer Slammer	www.spammerslammer.com

Security Applications

Security applications provide means of keeping private files and messages from prying eyes. These programs need to be used with caution, because they generally encrypt files so that a password is required to open them. If you forget the password, you won't be able to access those files yourself. Firewall programs in this category provide anti-hacking capability, to prevent hackers from accessing your PC while surfing you're the Internet.

Program	URL
ConSeal PC Firewall	www.signal9.com
DataSafe	www.authentex.com
Internet Firewall 98	www.digitalrobotics.com
PGP (Pretty Good Privacy)	www.nai.com
Secure Communicator	www.idirect.com/secure
ThunderSafe	www.ascit.com

Shareware Centers

For a wider range of shareware options, reviews of products, and quick access to downloads, visit any of the following Web sites with your Web browser:

Site Name	URL
5-Star Shareware	www.5star-shareware.com
Stroud's CWS Apps	http://cws.internet.com

Site Name	URL
TUCOWS	www.tucows.com
ZDNet Software Library	www.zdnet.com/swlib

Zip/Unzip Utilities

Many files that you download from the Internet will be *zipped* (compressed). These compressed files are generally smaller than the originals, and hence download more quickly. The following programs, available as shareware products, can be used both for zipping and unzipping compressed programs. Programs in this category are often referred to as *compression utilities* and *archive utilities*.

Program	URL
123Zip	www.atlastitan.com
AutoZip 98	www.mfsoft.com
CleverZip	www.cleverness.com
Drag and Zip	www.canyonsw.com
E-MailZip Deluxe	www.pepsoft.com
FileWrangler	www.cursorarts.com
PKZip for Windows	www.pkware.com
WinZip	www.winzip.com

USING WINZIP

When installed on your PC, WinZip automatically adds itself to your shortcut (right-click) menu. So to compress one or more files, you just need to get to those files via the Windows My Computer, Windows Explorer, or Find. To compress a single file, right-click it and choose Add To Zip. To compress multiple files into a single file, select the files you want to zip using the standard Windows Ctrl+Click or Shift+Click method. Then right-click any one of the selected files and choose Add To Zip.

CONTINUED ➡

Unzipping files is even easier. Click (or double-click in Windows 95 or Windows 98 "Classic View") the icon for any .zip file on your PC. The WinZip program will open showing the names of all the files that are compressed within the zip file. Click the Extract button to decompress the files. You'll be given the option to choose a folder for the unzipped files.

Appendix B

First Aid for Common Problems

This Appendix provides quick solutions for common problems in accessing the Internet. For most people, the toughest challenge is just getting connected to your ISP, so many of the problems listed deal with that topic. This Appendix, of course, isn't your only troubleshooting resource. The troubleshooters built into Windows and Outlook Express, discussed in the first sections below, can also help you diagnose and solve many problems.

Troubleshooting Tools

The remainder of this Appendix lists common problems and error messages that appear on the screen when problems arise. Many of these problems can also be diagnosed and solved in step-by-step fashion using the Windows troubleshooters. For general problems with connecting to your ISP, try the Windows Modem troubleshooter:

1. Click the Windows Start button and choose Help.

2. Click the Contents tab in the Help window that opens.

3. Click the Troubleshooting book icon to open it.

4. Click the Windows 9x Troubleshooters book to open it.

5. Click Modem.

6. In the pane on the right side, choose whichever option best describes the problem you're having.

7. Scroll to the bottom of that list and click the Next button.

Exactly what happens next depends on the problem you're facing. In most cases, the troubleshooter will take you through a series of steps that, hopefully, will solve the problem.

Troubleshooting Outlook Express

For help with e-mail or newsgroup problems, use the Outlook Express troubleshooters:

1. Start Microsoft Outlook Express in the usual manner.

2. Choose Help ➤ Contents And Index from the Outlook Express menu bar.

3. Click the Troubleshooting book to open it.

4. Choose the *If you have trouble using Outlook Express* page.

In the right pane, choose whichever option best describes the problem you're having. Then follow the instructions that appear on the screen.

Installing Missing Windows Programs

The Microsoft programs described in the chapters in this book come free with Windows 98. But just because you have them, doesn't necessarily mean they're all installed on your PC. Any missing programs (or *components* as they're called) will need to be installed from your original Windows 98 CD-ROM or floppy disks. If Windows 98 came pre-installed on your computer, you should be able to install the components without the use of a CD or floppy disk. To install missing programs, follow these steps:

1. Close any programs and windows on your PC (don't forget to save any work in progress) to get to the Windows desktop.

2. Click the Start button and choose Settings ➤ Control Panel.

3. Open the icon named Add/Remove Programs.

4. Click the Windows Setup tab in the dialog box that opens, as shown in Figure B.1.

The dialog box shows components and groups of components that are available for installation. Check boxes next to the component names mean the following:

▶ Empty checkbox: The component is not installed.

▶ Checked box: The component is installed.

▶ Grayed check box: Some components in this category are installed.

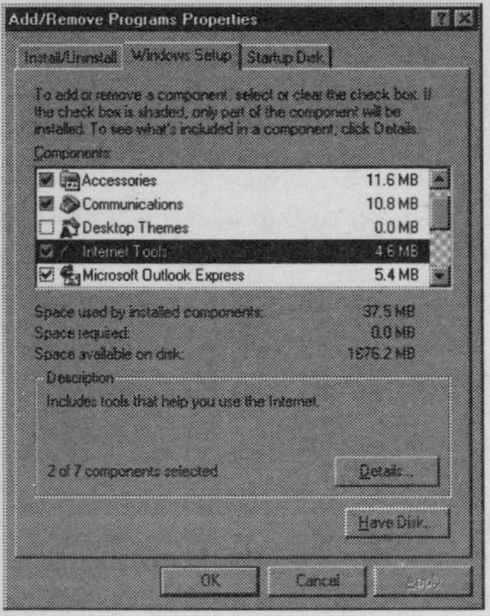

FIGURE B.1: The Windows Setup tab of Add/Remove Programs

Most of the components listed are actually groups of components. To see the individual components within a group, you first need to click the name of the group. For example, if you click the Internet Explorer group, then click the Details button and you'll see all the components in that category, as shown below.

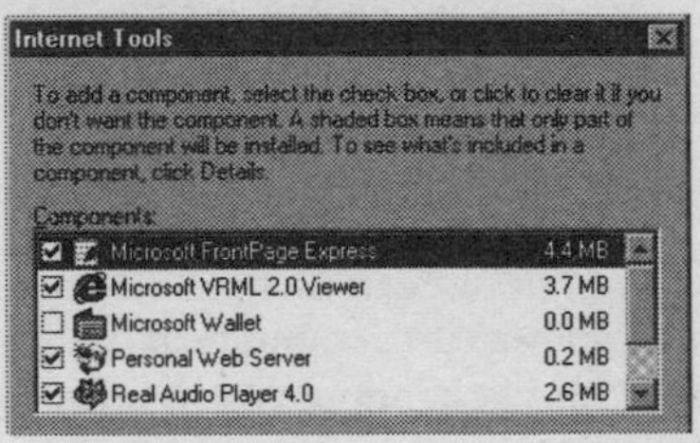

To install a component, you must first select its check box. You can select as many components as you wish. Be aware that de-selecting a component actually removes that component from your PC, so don't do so unless you're sure you want to remove that component. Table B.1 shows where the various programs described in this book are located.

TABLE B.1: Where Windows 98 Internet Programs are located

PROGRAM	WHERE LOCATED
Chat	Communications group
Dial-Up Networking	Communications group
Internet Explorer	(Always installed)
Outlook Express	On first list to appear

After selecting one or more components to install, click the OK button near the bottom of the dialog box. If you were inside a component group, you'll also need to click the OK button at the next dialog box to appear. After you click the final OK button, the installation will begin. Follow the instructions that appear on the screen, if any appear.

When the installation is complete and you get back to the Windows desktop, the newly-installed programs will be available from the Start menu. Click the Start button, choose Programs, and then choose Internet Explorer to see them.

NOTE

NetMeeting isn't available from Add/Remove Progams. You have to download NetMeeting from www.microsoft.com/netmeeting.

Windows 95 Internet

Windows 95 is a little trickier than Windows 98 because there were actually several versions of Windows 96 released to the public. Your best bet would be to explore all the components in the Windows Setup tab to see what's available for installation. If you can't find a component there, you can download it from the Internet. Go to Microsoft's Web site, particularly http://www.microsoft.com/msdownload or http://www.microsoft.com/ie.

If you have no way to get online to perform the download, your other option would be to buy the Internet Explorer version 4 (or version 5) program from your local computer store. However, if you were going to do that, you'd probably be better off just buying the upgrade kit to Windows 98. You'll get all the components described in this book, plus the better performance and wider range of capabilities that Windows 98 has to offer.

Common Problems

The remainder of this Appendix provides quick solutions to the most common problems beginners are faced with. For additional help, look to the built-in help for whatever program you happen to be using at the time. Just choose Help from that program's menu bar or press the Help key (the one labeled F1 at the top of the keyboard).

If you can't solve your connection problems using the information provided in this Appendix, your best bet is to contact your ISP. If you tell them that you're trying to connect using the Windows Dial-Up Networking program, they should be able to give you some specific solutions to your problem.

Call Is Cancelled before Connection Is Made

If your call is being cancelled before the connection to your ISP or online service is completed, follow these steps to allot more time:

1. Close any open messages and dialog boxes to get to the Windows desktop.

2. Click the Windows Start button and choose Settings ➢ Control Panel.

3. Open the Modems icon.

4. Click the name of the modem you use to dial into the your ISP.

5. Click the Properties button.

6. Click the Connection tab.

7. Select the *Cancel the call if not connected within x seconds* option and increase the time to 120 seconds or more, as shown below.

8. Click the OK button to close the Properties dialog box.

9. Click the Close button to close the Modems Properties dialog box.

Try your call again.

Can't Connect from Hotel/Building

If you're a mobile computerist, you may need to define a new location for each site you dial out from. Here's how:

1. Open the My Computer icon on the Windows desktop and then open the Dial-Up Networking icon.

2. Click (or double-click) the connectoid used to dial your ISP.

3. In the Connect To dialog box that appears, click the Dial Properties button.

4. Click the New button and then click OK in the little dialog box that appears.

5. Where it says New Location, type a new name for this connection (e.g., the name of the hotel or building you're dialing from).

6. Under Area Code, type the area code you're in right now.

7. If you need to dial a number to get an outside line, fill those numbers in under *To access an outside line*. For example, most hotels require dialing a 9 first for local calls and 8 for dialing long distance calls (or perhaps vice versa). The dialog box below shows how you'd type in those numbers.

Dialing Properties

My Locations

I am dialing from:
Drake Hotel, SF ▾   New...   Remove

I am in this country/region: Area code:
United States of America ▾   415   Area Code Rules...

When dialing from here

To access an outside line:
For local calls, dial   9
For long distance calls, dial   8

☐ To disable call waiting, dial ▾

Dial using: ◉ Tone dial   ○ Pulse dial

☐ For long distance calls, use this calling card:
None (Direct Dial) ▾   Calling Card...

Number to be dialed: 0 1 619 360-1900

OK   Cancel   Apply

TIP

If your ISP offers nationwide dialing numbers, you can avoid long-distance charges by choosing a phone number within your current area.

8. Click the OK button.

9. Make sure the Dialing From option in the Connect To dialog box reflects this new location. Then click the Connect button.

If the problem persists, try this:

1. Close all open programs and windows to get to the Windows desktop.

2. Open Internet Explorer.

3. In the Dial-Up Connection dialog box that appears, click the Settings button.

4. On the General tab, click the Use Area Code And Dialing Options checkbox, if it isn't already selected.

5. Click the OK button and then try again by clicking the Connect button.

Check Your Password...

If any error messages suggest checking your password, the first thing you need to do is check the username and password given to you by your ISP. It's important to keep in mind that usernames and passwords are often case-sensitive, which means that you need to type them using the exact upper and lowercase letters provided by your ISP.

If you type your password each time you log on, then you'll need to make sure the Caps Lock key is turned off and you're using the correct upper/lowercase letters each time you log on.

If you've chosen the Save Password option in the Connect To dialog box, then you need to make sure your stored username and password are typed correctly. Here's how:

1. Click the Windows Start button and choose Settings ➢ Control Panel.

2. Open the Internet icon.

3. Click the Connection tab.

4. Choose *Connect to the Internet using a modem* and then click the Settings button next to that option.

5. Select (drag the mouse pointer through) your user name and type it again, making sure you use the correct upper/lowercase letters. And make sure the Caps Lock key isn't on.

6. Select your password and re-type it, making sure to use the correct upper and lowercase letters.

7. Click the OK button to close the Dial-Up Settings dialog box and then click the OK button to close the Internet Properties dialog box.

Try connecting again. If the problem persists, you may need to check with your ISP to make sure you got the username and password right. And if you did, perhaps they can help you track down the real source of the problem.

Dial-Up Networking Can't Negotiate a Compatible Set of Protocols

If you see the above error message when you try to connect to your ISP, check your protocol settings. First click the OK button to dismiss the error message and then click the Cancel button in the Connect To dialog box. Then:

1. Open the My Computer icon on your Windows desktop and open the Dial-Up Networking icon.

2. Right-click the connectoid that you use to connect to your ISP and choose Properties.

3. Click the Server Types tab and choose options to match the shown in Figure B.2.

4. Click the OK button.

Follow the instructions that appear on the screen, if any. Then try connecting again.

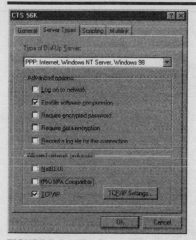

FIGURE B.2: The Server Types tab of a connectoid's properties

Error 678: The Computer You Are Dialing in to Is Not Answering

In some cases, the problem might indeed be with the computer that you're dialing into—though other problems will lead to the same error message. For example, if you've typed the dial-up phone number incorrectly, there may be no computer at the number to answer the phone. To check and correct the dial-up number:

1. Open the My Computer icon on your Windows desktop.

2. Open the Dial-Up Networking icon.

3. Right-click the icon for your Internet connectoid and choose Properties.

4. Double-check the area code and phone number shown in the dialog box and click the OK button.

If there was no problem with the phone number, the problem may be that your modem is disconnecting too quickly. Follow the steps under "Call is cancelled before connection is made" and "Dial-Up Networking can't negotiate a compatible set of protocols" above, and then try again.

Error 680: There Is No Dial Tone

As the message says, the modem can't dial because there is no dial tone. There could be several reasons for this:

▶ The Line jack on the modem is not connected to the phone jack on the wall.

▶ The modem is not turned on.

▶ Someone else is on the line, perhaps on a regular voice call.

▶ If you have voice mail, the tone used to alert you to new messages might be throwing the modem off. Check your messages and then make sure you get a normal dial tone when picking up the phone. If you get a normal dial tone, so will your modem.

▶ There is a problem with the phone line that the phone company needs to fix.

If you're travelling, you may need to define a new location with a dial-out number, as discussed under "Can't dial out from hotel/building" in this Appendix.

HTTP:1.0: Error 404

This error message appears when you try to visit a non-existent Web site or a Web site that's no longer available at that URL. Carefully check the URL in the Address bar of Internet Explorer to make sure you typed the URL correctly. A simple spelling error will prevent you from reaching the site.

Note that if the URL contains slashes, you need to type forward slashes, like this:

```
http://www.coolnerds.com/search
```

not like this:

```
http:\\www.coolnerds.com\search
```

Then press Enter and try again.

If that doesn't work and you're typing a lengthy URL, try going to the site's home page. To do so, just type the http://www .*whatever*.com part of the address without any trailing text and press the Enter key again.

Remember that not *all* URLs end in .com. If the URL ends in .net or .org or .edu, or whatever, make sure you've typed that correctly.

Internet Connection Wizard Disappeared

Once you've completed the Internet Connection Wizard, its icon changes to an Internet Explorer icon. If you need to run the connection Wizard again, try clicking the Start button and choosing Programs ➤ Internet Explorer ➤ Connection Wizard.

If the Connection Wizard option isn't available on the menu, try this approach instead:

1. Click the Start button and choose Settings ➤ Control Panel.

2. Open the Internet icon.

3. Click the Connection tab.

4. Click the Connect button near the top of the dialog box.

One approach or the other should do the trick.

Internet Explorer Never Connects to My ISP

If Internet Explorer doesn't dial into your ISP when starting and doesn't offer to let you dial in, your "Work Offline" option is probably activated. To fix that:

1. If you haven't already done so, open Microsoft Internet Explorer.

2. Choose File from Internet Explorer's menu bar.

3. If the Work Offline option has a check mark next to it, select that option to de-activate it.

4. Choose File ➢ Close from Internet Explorer's menu bar (do not click the Close (X) button).

5. Re-start Internet Explorer.

You should either be connected automatically or should see the Dial-Up Connection dialog box. If you do want to have Internet Explorer dial in without asking your permission, select the *Save password* and *Connect automatically* options. Then click the Connect button to connect.

It Always Makes Me Type My Password

If you share a computer with other people and you don't want them using your Internet account, then it makes sense to type your password each time you connect to your ISP. But if you're not worried about other people using your Internet account, you might as well just let your Dial-Up Networking connectoid type the password for you. To do so, follow the steps under "Internet Explorer doesn't connect automatically" above and select (check) the Save Password option.

Internet Subscriptions Don't Update Automatically

If you've subscribed to some Web sites, but Internet Explorer doesn't seem to be checking those sites during the night, first keep in mind that subscription updating only occurs if you leave your computer and modem running at night. (You can turn off the monitor to conserve electricity.)

Also, follow the steps below to make sure Internet Explorer is configured to automatically check subscriptions:

1. Start Microsoft Internet Explorer and choose View ➢ Internet Options from its menu bar.

2. Click the Advanced tab.

3. Select the *Enable scheduled subscription updates* option so its checkbox is checked.

4. Click the OK button to close the dialog box.

No Dial Tone

See "Error 680: There is no dial tone."

Appendix C

Top Tips for the Harried

I suppose many of you are in a hurry to get online, start browsing the Web, and perhaps start doing e-mail. If you have some basic Windows skills already and you don't feel like reading a whole lot of pages before you get started, this brief Appendix may be all you need to get started.

Do You Have a Modem?

If your computer already has a modem built in, or you've already purchased and installed a modem, you just need to make sure that the Line jack on the modem is connected to a telephone outlet on the wall. If you want to use that same phone number for a regular telephone, you also need to connect the Phone jack on the modem to the telephone. Then you can go straight to the section titled "Setting Up an Account" below.

If your computer has no modem, then purchasing a modem will be the first order of business. I suggest you purchase any Windows-compatible 56K modem that supports the V.90 standard. They're available at any computer store. You might want to take along your PC's system unit (the big boxy part—not the monitor, mouse, keyboard etc.—with you). Have the dealer install the modem for you to save additional time and headaches. When you get the PC with modem home, connect it to the phone jack on the wall, and perhaps the telephone, as described in the preceding paragraph.

If you need help with all of that, see Chapter 2.

Setting Up an Account

If you don't already have an Internet account, or an account with an online service like America Online or MSN, the quickest and easiest way to set one up is through the Internet Connection Wizard. To start the Wizard, choose one of the following methods:

▶ Open the Connect To The Internet icon on the Windows desktop.

▶ Click the Windows Start button and choose Programs ≻ Internet Explorer ≻ Internet Explorer ≻ Connection Wizard.

▶ Click the Internet Explorer icon on the Windows desktop.

Once the Internet Connection Wizard starts, follow the instructions that appear on the screen. If you need help, see Chapter 3.

Browsing the World Wide Web

If you want to visit a specific Web site and you know its URL (i.e., its www.*whatever*.com address), here's how you can get to that site:

1. Click the Internet Explorer icon on the Windows desktop or click the Start button and choose Programs ≻ Internet Explorer ≻ Internet Explorer.

2. If a dialog box titled Dial-up Connection appears, click its Connect button. Wait for the Dialing Progress dialog box that appears to disappear.

3. Initially, you'll be taken to Microsoft's Web page.

4. To visit another site, click in the Address bar and type in the URL of the site you want to visit. For example, below the Address bar is filled in to visit http://www.coolnerds.com.

5. Press Enter.

It may take a couple of minutes for the page you're visiting to appear on the screen. For more information on browsing the World Wide Web, see Chapters 5, 6, and 7.

E-Mail

To do e-mail on the Internet, use the Outlook Express program. To start that program, choose one of the following methods:

- ▶ Click the Outlook Express icon on the Windows desktop or Quick Launch toolbar.

- ▶ Click the Windows Start button and choose Programs ➤ Internet Explorer ➤ Outlook Express.

If you see a "Connecting to..." dialog box, wait for it to disappear. To create an e-mail message, click the Compose Message button on the Outlook Express toolbar. Type in the e-mail address, a subject, and your message, as in the example below. In that example the person sending the message has addressed it to `alan@coolnerds.com` (which is my e-mail address).

When you're ready to send the message, click the Send button that's just above the To: line where you typed the recipient's e-mail address.

If you see a message indicating that the message will not be sent right away, choose OK. Then choose Tools ➤ Send And Receive ➤ Send All from the Outlook Express menu bar.

To check your incoming mail, click the Send And Receive button on the Outlook Express toolbar. Wait for all the messages to be downloaded to your PC. When that job is done, click the Inbox folder in the left pane. Any new messages will be listed in the top right pane. The ones in boldface are ones you haven't read yet. To read a message, click its line in the top pane. The body of the message will appear in the lower pane.

To reply to the message, click the Reply To Author button in the toolbar. Type your message just above the original message and click the Send button, just as you would when sending a new message. If you have any problems or want to learn more about doing e-mail on the Internet, see Chapter 8.

Look at the Pictures

If you have a few spare minutes, you might want to just skim through the book and look at the pictures. You may be pleasantly surprised at just how much you learn. You may find answers to some of your own burning questions, pick up some of the jargon, and even pick up some useful tips.

Glossary

AOL   Short for America Online, a commercial online service that also provides access to the Internet.

applet   A small computer program, usually written in the Java programming language.

backbone   Generally a large cable that supports connections between many computers.

bandwidth   The amount of "stuff" a wire or cable can carry at a time. The higher the bandwidth, the faster the service.

bcc   Blind carbon copy. Prevents an e-mail recipient from seeing who else the message was addresses to.

bps   Bits per second, a measure of the speed of a modem or similar device. The higher the bps, the faster the device.

BRB   Be right back.

browser   Short for "Web browser," a program like Microsoft Internet Explorer or Netscape Navigator that lets you browse the World Wide Web.

BTW   By the way.

byte   The amount of storage required for a single character, like the letter "a" or "j."

cache   Pronounced like "cash," refers to a place in the computer used to store information. Your Internet cache stores recently-visited Web pages.

case-sensitive   Does not consider lowercase and uppercase letters to be the same. For example, "CAT" is not the same as "cat" when typing a case-sensitive password.

client   The computer on the receiving end of a client-server relationship. When you browse the Internet, your PC is an Internet client.

close button   The button marked "X "in the upper right corner of most program windows.

connectoid   The phone number and other settings that define how Dial-Up Networking connects to a particular network or ISP. Created automatically by the Internet Connection Wizard or manually using the Make New Connection icon within Dial-Up Networking.

default   A pre-selected setting that you can change or leave as is. Not indicative of a problem or "fault."

desktop   The main screen that appears when you first start Windows.

Dial-Up Networking   A Windows program that allows connections to networks via phone line. Open the Windows My Computer icon to locate its icon.

dialog box   A window that offers options for you to choose from.

directory   Another term for "folder," a place on a disk that holds its own collection of files.

domain name   The main name of a resource that's available on the Internet. For example, my domain name is coolnerds.com.

download   To copy a file from the Internet (or some other computer) to your own PC.

drag   To rest the mouse pointer on some item or selection and then hold down the primary mouse button while moving the mouse.

DUN   An abbreviation for Dial-Up Networking.

e-mail   Mail that's sent electronically across the Internet or a local area network.

emoticon   Characters typed to represent an emotion, such as the smiley– :-) used to represent "happy" or "only kidding."

extension   The ending part of a filename, such as .doc or .txt. Windows uses the extension to keep track of which documents go with which programs.

extranet   A network of computers used by two or more businesses that has the look and feel of the Internet.

FAQ   Frequently Asked Question.

file   A unit of storage on the disk. For example, any document you create and save will be stored in a file.

folder   A place on the hard disk where you can store files that belong together.

g or ‹g› or ‹gr›   Grin—used in e-mail messages and such to indicate "only kidding" or "no offense intended."

hard disk   A disk inside the PC that stores Windows, all your programs, and documents you save. Named C: on all PCs.

hardware   The PC itself, and any gadget you attach to the PC.

home page   The first page one comes to when visiting a Web site.

host   Any computer or device capable of providing services to other computers. Like the host at a party where all the guests are PCs.

HTML   Hypertext Markup Language, a set of codes used to define the appearance of Web pages. Learning to create Web pages requires learning about HTML.

hyperlink   A hot spot on a Web page that you can click to visit another Web page.

IMAP   Internet Message Access Protocol, an e-mail protocol that lets you manage messages without copying them from the server to your own PC.

IMHO   In my humble opinion.

install   To add a program to your computer's hard disk, usually by running its Setup program.

Internet   A huge network of interconnected computers from around the world. Provides popular services like e-mail and the World Wide Web.

Internet Service Provider   A company that can give you access to the Internet from your home or office. Abbreviated ISP.

intranet   a small local area network within an office or building that has the same look and feel as the Internet.

IRC   Internet Relay Chat, the protocol used for chatting on the Internet.

ISP   Short for Internet Service Provider, a business that can give you access to the Internet from your PC.

Java   A programming language used to create programs and small applets for Web pages.

K, Kb   An abbreviation for kilobyte.

kilobyte   About 1,000 bytes (1,024 to be exact).

LAN   Local Area Network, a small collection of interconected computers in an office or building.

link   Short for "hyperlink," a hot spot on a Web page that you can click to visit another Web page.

local   Your PC and anything that happens on your PC (as opposed to remote).

LOL   Laughing out loud.

M, Mb, meg   Abbreviation for megabyte.

maximize   To expand to full-screen size, either by clicking the Maximize button or double-clicking the title bar.

megabyte About a million bytes.

menu A list of options to choose from.

modem A gadget that connects your computer to a telephone line so you can use online services like the Internet.

monitor The part of a computer that looks like a television.

mouse pointer The little arrow or icon that moves on the screen as you roll the mouse around.

MSN Microsoft Network, a commercial online service that also offers Internet access.

NNTP Network News Transfer Protocol, used by Usenet Newsgroups.

OIC Oh, I see.

OTOH On the other hand.

point (mouse) To touch the mouse pointer to some item on the screen. (typography) A unit of measurement equal to approximately 1/72 inch.

pointer Short for "mouse pointer," the thing that moves on the screen as you roll the mouse.

POP Post Office Protocol, the protocol that defines how incoming messages are stored on your e-mail server.

POTS Plain Old Telephone System.

primary mouse button The button that's under your index finger when you rest your hand comfortably on the mouse, usually the left mouse button.

protocol The preferred or standard way of doing things. In computer terms, computers can only talk to each other if both follow the same protocols.

remote   Any computer other than your own "local" PC. The Internet gives you access to remote computers.

right-drag   To drag an item using the secondary (right) mouse button rather than the primary (left) mouse button.

ROTFL   Rolling on the floor laughing.

RTFM   Read the manual. (I've left out the "F" because we can't print that word in a book like this!)

server   A computer that sits on the Internet and "serves up" Web pages or other information to clients.

SMTP   Simple Mail Transfer Protocol, the protocol used for sending e-mail over the Internet.

spam   Junk mail. "Spamming" is using the Internet to send out junk e-mail.

Start button   The button labeled Start in the Windows 98 taskbar.

T1 thru T3   High-speed lines used by ISPs and large businesses to maintain a fast, full-time connection to the Internet.

taskbar   A bar that contains the Start button, indicators, and more. Generally appears along the bottom edge of the screen.

TIA   Thanks in advance.

upload   To copy a file from your PC to some other computer, perhaps a computer on the Internet.

URL   Uniform Resource Locator, the "address" of a Web site. For example, www.coolnerds.com is a URL.

WAN   A Wide Area Network, such as the Internet.

Web browser   A program that lets you visit Web sites on the Internet. Microsoft Internet Explorer is the browser that comes with Windows 98.

Web page A page of information stored on the Internet that anyone on the Internet can visit using their Web browser.

Web site A place on the Internet that you can visit using a Web browser. Each Web site has its own unique URL (address).

Web view A navigation option that lets you open icons by clicking them once.

Windows 98 Desktop The main screen you see after starting your PC and waiting for Windows to kick in.

Wizard Step-by-step instructions presented by Windows to make it easier to use more advanced features.

World Wide Web One of the most popular services of the Internet, home to all those www.*whatever*.com addresses.

INDEX

Note: Throughout this index *italics* page numbers refer to figures; **boldfaced** page numbers refer to primary discussions of the topic.

I